site pages, reproduced line for line and page for page. This is preceded by the translators' brief introduction and followed by a summary listing of the parallels between the new sayings and Biblical passages.

Upon the advice of the translator-editors, this most important portion of the rich Coptic material is the first to be released to the public in an unprecedented international publishing event, with conjoint publication in five languages and six editions.

With this first publication of THE GOSPEL ACCORDING TO THOMAS in Europe and America, a great number of interests will be served simultaneously. Among them:

1. A desire among the public to learn more of early Christianity and its setting.

2. Eagerness among the followers of the teachings of Jesus for more light on his actual sayings and influence.

3. The fascination of ancient manuscripts and archaeological discoveries aroused by the Dead Sea Scrolls and other recent findings.

THE GOSPEL ACCORDING TO THOMAS

THE GOSPEL
ACCORDING TO THOMAS

COPTIC TEXT ESTABLISHED AND TRANSLATED

BY

A. GUILLAUMONT, H.-CH. PUECH, G. QUISPEL,
W. TILL AND † YASSAH 'ABD AL MASĪḤ

LEIDEN
E. J. BRILL

NEW YORK
HARPER & BROTHERS

PRELIMINARY REMARKS

What follows is nothing more than a fragment of a work which is much more extensive and complete: a critical, scholarly edition of *The Gospel according to Thomas*, which will include a long introduction devoted to the various problems—philological, historical and exegetical—which have been raised by the document, as well as the Coptic text of the writing, a translation in German, French or English, a commentary consisting of detailed notes, and an index of Coptic and Greek terms. This volume will be published in the near future. In view, however, of certain technical difficulties which have delayed the printing and publication of the larger work, we think it wise to make available in advance this extract. *The Gospel according to Thomas* is a document so important, the announcement of its discovery and what has already been said concerning it have evoked so great a curiosity on the part of the general public and so great an interest on the part of the scholarly world, that it is impossible for us to delay its publication further or to decide otherwise.

By extracting this section of the coming edition and by publishing it beforehand, we have intended above all to furnish a preliminary working tool for purposes of instruction and research, so that our colleagues may proceed on the solid ground provided by the text itself, here transcribed and occasionally reconstructed, and may more easily judge its translation, which has been made as literal as possible.

The numerals which appear at the top and in the margin of the left-hand pages refer to the plates of the photographic edition of the manuscript, which we owe to Dr. Pahor Labib

(*Coptic Gnostic Papyri in the Coptic Museum at Old Cairo*, vol. I, Cairo 1956, pl. 80, line 10-pl. 99, line 28). The numerals which appear at the top of the right-hand pages, or have been inserted within parentheses on these pages, correspond to the numbers of the 114 *logia*, which represent our enumeration within this collection of "Sayings of Jesus", which comprise almost exclusively the present "Gospel".

The critical apparatus and the notes refer only to the constitution and the primary interpretation of the text. A summary list of scriptural parallels or echoes has been added in the form of an appendix. The variants, the extra-canonical parallels, the testimonies of the indirect tradition relative to this or that *logion*, the Semitisms which here or there lie beneath the surface, and other analogies, will be expounded in the commentary of the authoritative edition.

The manuscript, now preserved in the Coptic Museum of Old Cairo, has been collated there, in October 1956, by three of us. It belongs to one of the thirteen volumes which together form the Gnostic library found, about 1945, in the neighborhood of Nag-Hamâdi (Upper Egypt); this volume is Codex III of our classification. The Codex must probably be dated either in the second half of the Fourth Century A.D. or in the beginning of the Fifth Century A.D. But the original of *The Gospel according to Thomas*—the second of the seven writings contained in this volume—goes back much earlier. We are dealing here with a translation or an adaptation in Sahidic Coptic of a work the primitive text of which must have been produced in Greek about 140 A.D., and which was based on even more ancient sources.

The English text of this edition has been read by Paul S. Minear of Yale University Divinity School.

For further details see:

H.-Ch. Puech, Une collection de Paroles de Jésus récemment retrouvée: L'Évangile selon Thomas, in *Comptes Rendus de l'Académie des Inscriptions et Belles-Lettres* (Institut de France), 1957, pp. 146-167.

H.-Ch. Puech, Das Thomas-Evangelium, in E. Hennecke-W. Schneemelcher, *Neutestamentliche Apokryphen*[3], t. I, Tübingen, 1959, pp. 199-223.

G. Quispel, The Gospel of Thomas and the New Testament, in *Vigiliae Christianae*, XI, 1957, pp. 189-207.

G. Quispel, L'Évangile selon Thomas et les Clémentines, *ibid.*, XII, 1958, pp. 181-196.

A. Guillaumont, Sémitismes dans les logia de Jésus retrouvés à Nag-Hamâdi, in *Journal Asiatique*, CCXLVI, 1958, pp. 113-123.

W. C. Till, New Sayings of Jesus in the Recently Discovered Coptic, "Gospel of Thomas", in *Bulletin of the John Rylands Library* XLI, 1959, pp. 446-458.

THE GOSPEL ACCORDING TO THOMAS

80 10 ⲛⲁⲉⲓ ⲛⲉ ⲛ̄ϣⲁϫⲉ ⲉⲑⲏⲡ ⲉⲛⲧⲁⲓⲥ ⲉⲧⲟⲛϩ
ϫⲟⲟⲩ ⲁⲩⲱ ⲁϥⲥϩⲁⲓ̈ⲥⲟⲩ ⲛ̄ϭⲓ ⲇⲓⲇⲩⲙⲟⲥ

12 ⲓ̈ⲟⲩⲇⲁⲥ ⲑⲱⲙⲁⲥ (1) ⲁⲩⲱ ⲡⲉϫⲁϥ ϫⲉ ⲡⲉ
ⲧⲁϩⲉ ⲉⲑⲉⲣⲙⲏⲛⲉⲓⲁ ⲛ̄ⲛⲉⲉⲓϣⲁϫⲉ ϥⲛⲁ

14 ϫⲓ †ⲡⲉ ⲁⲛ ⲙ̄ⲡⲙⲟⲩ (2) ⲡⲉϫⲉ ⲓ̄ⲥ ⲙ̄ⲛⲧⲣⲉϥ
ⲗⲟ ⲛ̄ϭⲓ ⲡⲉⲧϣⲓⲛⲉ ⲉϥϣⲓⲛⲉ ϣⲁⲛⲧⲉϥ

16 ϭⲓⲛⲉ ⲁⲩⲱ ϩⲟⲧⲁⲛ ⲉϥϣⲁⲛϭⲓⲛⲉ ϥⲛⲁ
ϣⲧⲣ̄ⲧⲣ̄ ⲁⲩⲱ ⲉϥϣⲁⲛϣⲧⲟⲣⲧⲣ̄ ϥⲛⲁⲣ̄

18   (blank)   ϣⲡⲏⲣⲉ ⲁⲩⲱ ϥⲛⲁⲣ̄
ⲣ̄ⲣⲟ ⲉϫ̄ⲙ ⲡⲧⲏⲣϥ (3) ⲡⲉϫⲉ ⲓ̄ⲥ ϫⲉ ⲉⲩϣⲁ

20 ϫⲟⲟⲥ ⲛⲏⲧⲛ̄ ⲛ̄ϭⲓ ⲛⲉⲧⲥⲱⲕ ϩⲏⲧ ⲧⲏⲩⲧⲛ̄
ϫⲉ ⲉⲓⲥ ϩⲏⲏⲧⲉ ⲉⲧⲙ̄ⲛⲧⲉⲣⲟ ϩⲛ̄ ⲧⲡⲉ ⲉ

22 ⲉⲓⲉ ⲛ̄ϩⲁⲗⲏⲧ ⲛⲁⲣ̄ ϣⲟⲣⲡ̄ ⲉⲣⲱⲧⲛ̄ ⲛ̄ⲧⲉ
ⲧⲡⲉ ⲉⲩϣⲁⲛϫⲟⲟⲥ ⲛⲏⲧⲛ̄ ϫⲉ ⲥϩⲛ̄ ⲑⲁ

24 ⲗⲁⲥⲥⲁ ⲉⲉⲓⲉ ⲛ̄ⲧⲃⲧ̄ ⲛⲁⲣ̄ ϣⲟⲣⲡ̄ ⲉⲣⲱⲧⲛ̄
ⲁⲗⲗⲁ ⲧⲙⲛ̄ⲧⲉⲣⲟ ⲥⲙ̄ⲡⲉⲧⲛ̄ϩⲟⲩⲛ̄ ⲁⲩⲱ

26 ⲥⲙ̄ⲡⲉⲧⲛ̄ⲃⲁⲗ ϩⲟⲧⲁⲛ ⲉⲧⲉⲧⲛ̄ϣⲁⲛ
ⲥⲟⲩⲱⲛ ⲧⲏⲩⲧⲛ̄ ⲧⲟⲧⲉ ⲥⲉⲛⲁⲥⲟⲩ

81 ⲧⲏⲛⲉ ⲁⲩⲱ ⲧⲉⲧⲛⲁⲉⲓⲙⲉ ϫⲉ ⲛ̄ⲧⲱⲧⲛ̄ ⲡⲉ

2 ⲛ̄ϣⲏⲣⲉ ⲙ̄ⲡⲉⲓⲱⲧ ⲉⲧⲟⲛϩ ⲉϣⲱⲡⲉ ⲇⲉ
ⲧⲉⲧⲛⲁⲥⲟⲩⲱⲛ ⲧⲏⲩⲧⲛ̄ ⲁⲛ ⲉⲉⲓⲉ ⲧⲉⲧⲛ̄

4 ϣⲟⲟⲡ ϩⲛ̄ ⲟⲩⲙⲛ̄ⲧϩⲏⲕⲉ ⲁⲩⲱ ⲛ̄ⲧⲱⲧⲛ̄
ⲡⲉ ⲧⲙⲛ̄ⲧϩⲏⲕⲉ (4) ⲡⲉϫⲉ ⲓ̄ⲥ ϥⲛⲁϫⲛⲁⲩ ⲁⲛ

6 ⲛ̄ϭⲓ ⲡⲣⲱⲙⲉ ⲛ̄ϩⲗ̄ⲗⲟ ϩⲛ̄ ⲛⲉϥϩⲟⲟⲩ ⲉϫⲛⲉ
ⲟⲩⲕⲟⲩⲉⲓ ⲛ̄ϣⲏⲣⲉ ϣⲏⲙ ⲉϥϩⲛ̄ ⲥⲁϣϥ̄

8 ⲛ̄ϩⲟⲟⲩ ⲉⲧⲃⲉ ⲡⲧⲟⲡⲟⲥ ⲙ̄ⲡⲱⲛϩ ⲁⲩⲱ
ϥⲛⲁⲱⲛϩ ϫⲉ ⲟⲩⲛ̄ ϩⲁϩ ⲛ̄ϣⲟⲣⲡ̄ ⲛⲁⲣ̄ ϩⲁ

80 10 These are the secret words which the Living Jesus
spoke and Didymos Judas Thomas wrote.

12 (1) And He said :
Whoever finds the explanation (ἑρμηνεία) of these words will

14 not taste death. (2) Jesus said :
Let him who seeks, not cease seeking until he

16 finds, and when (ὅταν) he finds, he will
be troubled, and when he has been troubled, he will

18 marvel and he will
reign over the All. (3) Jesus said : If

20 those who lead you say to you :
"See, the Kingdom is in heaven",

22 then the birds of the heaven will precede you .
If they say to you : "It is in the sea (θάλασσα),"

24 then the fish will precede you .
But (ἀλλά) the Kingdom is within you and

26 it is without you. If (ὅταν) you (will)
know yourselves, then (τότε) you will be known

81 and you will know that you are

2 the sons of the Living Father. But (δέ) if
you do not know yourselves, then you

4 are in poverty and you
are poverty. (4) Jesus said : The man old in days will not

6 hesitate to ask
a little child of seven

8 days about the place (τόπος) of Life, and
he will live. For many who are first shall become last

3

10 ⲉ ⲁⲩⲱ ⲛ̄ⲥⲉϣⲱⲡⲉ ⲟⲩⲁ ⲟⲩⲱⲧ (5) ⲡⲉϫⲉ ⲓ̄ⲥ̄
ⲥⲟⲩⲱⲛ ⲡⲉⲧⲙ̄ⲡⲙ̄ⲧⲟ ⲙ̄ⲡⲉⲕϩⲟ ⲉⲃⲟⲗ`

12 ⲁⲩⲱ ⲡⲉⲑⲏⲡ` ⲉⲣⲟⲕ` ϥⲛⲁϭⲱⲗⲡ` ⲉⲃⲟⲗ
ⲛⲁⲕ` ⲙⲛ̄ ⲗⲁⲁⲩ ⲅⲁⲣ ⲉϥϩⲏⲡ` ⲉϥⲛⲁⲟⲩⲱⲛϩ

14 ⲉⲃⲟⲗ ⲁⲛ (6) ⲁⲩϫⲛⲟⲩϥ ⲛ̄ϭⲓ ⲛⲉϥ`ⲙⲁⲑⲏⲧⲏⲥ
ⲡⲉϫⲁⲩ ⲛⲁϥ ϫⲉ ⲕ`ⲟⲩⲱϣ ⲉⲧⲣⲏⲣⲛⲏⲥⲧⲉⲩⲉ

16 ⲁⲩⲱ ⲉϣ ⲧⲉ ⲑⲉ ⲉⲛⲁϣⲗ̄ⲗ ⲉⲛⲁϯ ⲉⲗⲉ
ⲏⲙⲟⲥⲩⲛⲏ ⲁⲩⲱ ⲉⲛⲁⲣ̄ⲡⲁⲣⲁⲧⲏⲣⲉⲓ ⲉⲟⲩ

18 ⲛ̄ϭⲓⲟⲩⲱⲙ` ⲡⲉϫⲉ ⲓ̄ⲥ̄ ϫⲉ ⲙ̄ⲡⲣ̄ϫⲉ ϭⲟⲗ ⲁⲩ
ⲱ ⲡⲉⲧⲉⲧⲙ̄ⲙⲟⲥⲧⲉ ⲙ̄ⲙⲟϥ` ⲙ̄ⲡⲣⲁⲁϥ ϫⲉ

20 ⲥⲉϭⲟⲗⲡ` ⲧⲏⲣⲟⲩ ⲉⲃⲟⲗ ⲙ̄ⲡⲉⲙⲧⲟ ⲉⲃⲟⲗ
ⲛ̄ⲧⲡⲉ ⲙⲛ̄ ⲗⲁⲁⲩ ⲅⲁⲣ ⲉϥϩⲏⲡ` ⲉϥⲛⲁⲟⲩ

22 ⲱⲛϩ ⲉⲃⲟⲗ ⲁⲛ ⲁⲩⲱ ⲙⲛ̄ ⲗⲁⲁⲩ ⲉϥϩⲟⲃⲥ̄ ⲉⲩ
ⲛⲁϭⲱ ⲟⲩⲉϣⲛ̄ ϭⲟⲗⲡϥ` (7) ⲡⲉϫⲉ ⲓ̄ⲥ̄ ⲟⲩ

24 ⲙⲁⲕⲁⲣⲓⲟⲥ ⲡⲉ ⲡⲙⲟⲩⲉⲓ ⲡⲁⲉⲓ ⲉⲧⲉ
ⲡⲣⲱⲙⲉ ⲛⲁⲟⲩⲟⲙϥ ⲁⲩⲱ ⲛ̄ⲧⲉⲡⲙⲟⲩⲉⲓ

26 ϣⲱⲡⲉ ⲣ̄ⲣⲱⲙⲉ ⲁⲩⲱ ϥⲃⲏⲧ` ⲛ̄ϭⲓ ⲡⲣⲱ
ⲙⲉ ⲡⲁⲉⲓ ⲉⲧⲉ ⲡⲙⲟⲩⲉⲓ ⲛⲁⲟⲩⲟⲙϥ ⲁⲩ

28 ⲱ ⲡⲙⲟⲩⲉⲓ ⲛⲁϣⲱⲡⲉ ⲣ̄ⲣⲱⲙⲉ (8) ⲁⲩⲱ ⲡⲉ
ϫⲁϥ ϫⲉ ⲉⲡⲣⲱⲙⲉ ⲧⲏⲧⲱⲛ ⲁⲩⲟⲩⲱϩⲉ

30 ⲣ̄ⲣⲙ̄ⲛ̄ϩⲏⲧ` ⲡⲁⲉⲓ ⲛ̄ⲧⲁϩⲛⲟⲩϫⲉ ⲛ̄ⲧⲉϥϥ
ⲃⲱ ⲉⲑⲁⲗⲁⲥⲥⲁ ⲁϥⲥⲱⲕ ⲙ̄ⲙⲟⲥ ⲉϩⲣⲁⲓ

32 ϩⲛ̄ ⲑⲁⲗⲁⲥⲥⲁ ⲉⲥⲙⲉϩ ⲛ̄ⲧⲃ̄ⲧ ⲛ̄ⲕⲟⲩⲉⲓ ⲛ̄
ϩⲣⲁⲓ ⲛ̄ϩⲏⲧⲟⲩ ⲁϥϩⲉ ⲁⲩⲛⲟϭ ⲛ̄ⲧⲃ̄ⲧ ⲉⲛⲁ

---

21 ⲛ̄ⲧⲡⲉ *sic*; *l.* ⲛ̄ⲧⲙⲉ?

28 *sic*; *l.* ⲡⲣⲱⲙⲉ ⲛⲁϣⲱⲡⲉ ⲙ̄ⲙⲟⲩⲉⲓ

4

10 and they shall become a single one. (5) Jesus said:
Know what is in thy sight,

12 and what is hidden from thee will be revealed
to thee. For (γάρ) there is nothing hidden which will

14 not be manifest. (6) His disciples (μαθητής) asked Him,
they said to Him: Wouldst thou that we fast (νηστεύειν),

16 and how should we pray (and) should we give alms (ἐλεημοσύνη),
and what diet should we observe (παρατηρεῖν)?

18 Jesus said: Do not lie;
and do not do what you hate, for

20 all things are manifest before Heaven.
For (γάρ) there is nothing hidden that shall not

22 be revealed and there is nothing covered that
shall remain without being uncovered. (7) Jesus said:

24 Blessed (μακάριος) is the lion which
the man eats and the lion

26 will become man; and cursed is the man
whom the lion eats and

28 the lion will become man. (8) And He said:
The Man is like a wise fisherman

30 who cast his net
into the sea (θάλασσα), he drew it up

32 from the sea (θάλασσα) full of small fish;
among them he found a large (and) good fish,

11 "what" or "him who".
15 read: "How wouldst thou".
20 "Heaven": perhaps originally "the Truth".
28 read: "the man will become lion".

5

34 нотӌ· ноɪ потѡрє ррмирнт· аӌноꙋ

ϫє ннкотєɪ тироꙋ нтвт· євоⲗ є[пє]

82 снт єѳаⲗасса аӌсѡтп· мпноб н

2 твт ҳѡрɪс рɪсє пєтє оꙋн мааϫє ммоӌ

єсѡтм марєӌ·сѡтм (9) пєҳє іс ϫє єɪс рн

4 нтє аӌєɪ євоⲗ ноɪ пєт·сɪтє аӌмєр тоотӌ

аӌноꙋϫє ароєɪнє мєн рє єϫн тєрɪн·

6 аꙋєɪ ноɪ нраⲗатє аꙋкатӌоꙋ рнкоотє

аꙋрє єϫн тпєтра аꙋѡ мпоꙋϫє ноꙋнє

8 єпєснт· єпкар аꙋѡ мпоꙋтєꙋє рмс єр

раї єтпє аꙋѡ рнкоотє аꙋрє єϫн нѱо

10 тє аꙋѡст· мпєхрос аꙋѡ апӌнт оꙋомоꙋ

аꙋѡ арнкоотє рє єϫн пкар єтнаноꙋӌ·

12 аꙋѡ аӌϯ карпос єрраї єтпє єнаноꙋӌ· аӌ

єɪ нсє єсотє аꙋѡ ѱє ϫоꙋѡт· єсотє

14 (10) пєϫє іс ϫє аєɪноꙋϫє ноꙋкѡрт· єϫн

пкосмос аꙋѡ єɪс рннтє ϯарєр єроӌ·

16 ѱантєӌϫєро (11) пєϫє іс ϫє тєєɪпє нарпа

ратє аꙋѡ тєтнпє ммос нарпаратє

18 аꙋѡ нєтмооꙋт сєонр ан аꙋѡ нєтонр

сєнамоꙋ ан нрооꙋ нєтєтноꙋѡм·

20 мпєтмооꙋт· нєтєтнєɪрє ммоӌ мпє

тонр ротан єтєтнѱанѱѡпє рм поꙋ

22 оєɪн оꙋ пєтєтнааӌ рм фооꙋ єтєтн

12/13 аӌєɪ for аӌӌɪ?

14 аєɪноꙋϫє perhaps for аєɪєɪ єноꙋϫє?

19 нєтєтн *sic; l.* єнєтєтн

14 the stones and burn you up.

(14) Jesus said to them: If you fast (νηστεύειν), you will

16 beget sin for yourselves, and if you

pray, you will be condemned (κατακρίνειν), and

18 if you give alms (ἐλεημοσύνη), you will do

evil (κακόν) to your spirits (πνεῦμα). And if you

20 go into any land and

wander in the regions (χώρα), if they receive (παραδέχεσθαι)

22 you, eat what they set before you,

heal (θεραπεύειν) the sick among them.

24 For (γάρ) what goes into your mouth

will not defile you, but (ἀλλά) what

26 comes out of your mouth, that is what

will defile you. (15) Jesus said: When (ὅταν)

28 you see Him who was not born

of woman, prostrate yourselves upon

30 your face and adore Him: He

is your Father. (16) Jesus said:

32 Men possibly (τάχα) think that I have come to throw

peace (εἰρήνη) upon the world (κόσμος) and

34 they do not know that I have come to throw

divisions upon the earth, fire, sword,

36 war (πόλεμος). For (γάρ) there shall be five

84 in a house: three shall be against

2 two and two against three, the father

against the son and the son against the father,

4 ⲁⲩⲱ ⲥⲉⲛⲁⲱϩⲉ ⲉⲣⲁⲧⲟⲩ ⲉⲧⲟ ⲙ̄ⲙⲟⲛⲁ

ⲭⲟⲥ (17) ⲡⲉⲭⲉ ⲓ̄ⲥ̄ ϫⲉ ϯⲛⲁϯ ⲛⲏⲧⲛ̄ ⲙ̄ⲡⲉⲧⲉ

6 ⲙ̄ⲡⲉⲃⲁⲗ ⲛⲁⲩ ⲉⲣⲟϥ ⲁⲩⲱ ⲡⲉⲧⲉ ⲙ̄ⲡⲉⲙⲁ

ⲁϫⲉ ⲥⲟⲧⲙⲉϥ· ⲁⲩⲱ ⲡⲉⲧⲉ ⲙ̄ⲡⲉϭⲓϫ ϭⲙ̄

8 ϭⲱⲙϥ· ⲁⲩⲱ ⲙ̄ⲡⲉϥⲉⲓ ⲉϩⲣⲁⲓ̈ ϩⲓ ⲫⲏⲧ·

ⲣ̄ⲣⲱⲙⲉ (18) ⲡⲉϫⲉ ⲙ̄ⲙⲁⲑⲏⲧⲏⲥ ⲛ̄ⲓ̄ⲥ̄ ϫⲉ ϫⲟ

10 ⲟⲥ ⲉⲣⲟⲛ ϫⲉ ⲧⲛ̄ϩⲁⲏ ⲉⲥⲛⲁϣⲱⲡⲉ ⲛ̄

ⲁϣ ⲛ̄ϩⲉ ⲡⲉϫⲉ ⲓ̄ⲥ̄ ⲁⲧⲉⲧⲛ̄ϭⲱⲗⲡ· ⲅⲁⲣ ⲉⲃⲟⲗ

12 ⲛ̄ⲧⲁⲣⲭⲏ ϫⲉⲕⲁⲁⲥ ⲉⲧⲉⲧⲛⲁϣⲓⲛⲉ ⲛ̄ⲥⲁ

ⲑⲁϩⲏ ϫⲉ ϩⲙ̄ ⲡⲙⲁ ⲉⲧⲉ ⲧⲁⲣⲭⲏ ⲙ̄ⲙⲁⲩ ⲉ

14 ⲑⲁϩⲏ ⲛⲁϣⲱⲡⲉ ⲙ̄ⲙⲁⲩ ⲟⲩⲙⲁⲕⲁⲣⲓⲟⲥ

ⲡⲉⲧⲛⲁⲱϩⲉ ⲉⲣⲁⲧϥ̄ ϩⲛ̄ ⲧⲁⲣⲭⲏ ⲁⲩⲱ

16 ϥⲛⲁⲥⲟⲩⲱⲛ ⲑⲁⲏ ⲁⲩⲱ ϥⲛⲁϫⲓ ϯⲡⲉ

ⲁⲛ ⲙ̄ⲙⲟⲩ (19) ⲡⲉϫⲉ ⲓ̄ⲥ̄ ϫⲉ ⲟⲩⲙⲁⲕⲁⲣⲓⲟⲥ

18 ⲡⲉ ⲛ̄ⲧⲁϩϣⲱⲡⲉ ϩⲁⲧⲉϩⲏ ⲉⲙⲡⲁⲧⲉϥϣⲱ

ⲡⲉ ⲉⲧⲉⲧⲛ̄ϣⲁⲛϣⲱⲡⲉ ⲛⲁⲉⲓ ⲙ̄ⲙⲁⲑⲏ

20 ⲧⲏⲥ ⲛ̄ⲧⲉⲧⲛ̄ⲥⲱⲧⲙ̄ ⲁⲛⲁϣⲁϫⲉ ⲛⲉⲉⲓⲱ

ⲛⲉ ⲛⲁⲣ̄ⲇⲓⲁⲕⲟⲛⲉⲓ ⲛⲏⲧⲛ̄ ⲟⲩⲛ̄ⲧⲏⲧⲛ̄

22 ⲅⲁⲣ ⲙ̄ⲙⲁⲩ ⲛ̄ⲧⲟⲩ ⲛ̄ϣⲏⲛ ϩⲙ̄ ⲡⲁⲣⲁ·

ⲇⲓⲥⲟⲥ ⲉⲥⲉⲕⲓⲙ ⲁⲛ ⲛ̄ϣⲱⲙ· ⲙ̄ⲡⲣⲱ

13 and 14 ⲑⲁϩⲏ, 16 ⲑⲁⲏ *sic*; *l.* ⲑⲁⲏ or ⲧϩⲁⲏ

15 after ⲡⲉⲧⲛⲁ there is ϩ deleted by a horizontal stroke. It looks like Achmi-
mic ϩ . But as this is not found in our text it cannot be ϩ = S ϣ 'to
be able'

22 ⲡⲁⲣⲁ *sic*; *l.* ⲡⲡⲁⲣⲁ

23 ⲉⲥⲉⲕⲓⲙ for classical Sahidic ⲉⲛⲥⲉⲕⲓⲙ

12

4 and they will stand as solitaries (μοναχός).

(17) Jesus said: I will give you what

6 eye has not seen and what ear

has not heard and what hand has not touched

8 and (what) has not arisen in the heart

of man. (18) The disciples (μαθητής) said to Jesus: Tell

10 us how our end will be.

Jesus said: Have you then (γάρ) discovered

12 the beginning (ἀρχή) so that you inquire about

the end? For where the beginning (ἀρχή) is,

14 there shall be the end. Blessed (μακάριος) is

he who shall stand at the beginning (ἀρχή), and

16 he shall know the end and he shall not taste

death. (19) Jesus said: Blessed (μακάριος) is

18 he who was before he came into being.

If you become disciples (μαθητής) to Me

20 and hear My words, these stones

will minister (διακονεῖν) to you.

22 For (γάρ) you have five trees in Paradise (παράδεισος),

which are unmoved in summer (or) in winter

24 ⲁⲧⲱ ⲙⲁⲣⲉⲛⲟⲧⲟⲱⲃⲉ ϩⲉ ⲉⲃⲟⲗ ⲡⲉⲧ·

ⲛⲁⲥⲟⲧⲱⲛⲟⲧ ϥⲛⲁϫⲓ ϯⲡⲉ ⲁⲛ· ⲙⲙⲟⲧ

26 (20) ⲡⲉϫⲉ ⲙⲙⲁⲑⲏⲧⲏⲥ ⲛⲓⲥ ϫⲉ ϫⲟⲟⲥ

ⲉⲣⲟⲛ ϫⲉ ⲧⲙⲛⲧⲉⲣⲟ ⲛⲙⲡⲏⲧⲉ ⲉⲥ

28 ⲧⲏⲧⲱⲛ ⲉⲛⲓⲙ ⲡⲉϫⲁϥ ⲛⲁⲧ ϫⲉ ⲉⲥⲧⲛ

ⲧⲱⲛ ⲁⲧⲃⲗⲃⲓⲗⲉ ⲛϣⲗⲧⲁⲙ ⲥⲟⲃⲕ ⲡⲁ

30 ⲣⲁ ⲛϭⲣⲟϭ ⲧⲏⲣⲟⲧ ϩⲟⲧⲁⲛ ⲇⲉ ⲉⲥϣⲁ

ϩⲉ ⲉϫⲙ ⲡⲕⲁϩ ⲉⲧⲟⲩⲣ ϩⲱⲃ ⲉⲣⲟϥ ϣⲁϥ

32 ⲧⲉⲟⲧ ⲉⲃⲟⲗ ⲛⲛⲟⲧⲛⲟϭ ⲛⲧⲁⲣ ⲛϥϣⲱ

ⲡⲉ ⲛⲥⲕⲉⲡⲏ ⲛϩⲁⲗⲁⲧⲉ ⲛⲧⲡⲉ (21) ⲡⲉ

34 ϫⲉ ⲙⲁⲣⲓϩⲁⲙ ⲛⲓⲥ ϫⲉ ⲉⲛⲉⲕⲙⲁⲑⲏ

ⲧⲏⲥ ⲉⲓⲛⲉ ⲛⲛⲓⲙ ⲡⲉϫⲁϥ ϫⲉ ⲉⲧⲉⲓⲛⲉ

85 ⲛϩⲛϣⲏⲣⲉ ϣⲏⲙ ⲉⲧ[ϭ]ⲉⲗⲓⲧ ⲁⲧⲥⲱϣⲉ ⲉⲧⲱ

2 ⲟⲧ ⲁⲛ ⲧⲉ ϩⲟⲧⲁⲛ ⲉⲧϣⲁⲉⲓ ⲛϭⲓ ⲛϫⲟⲉⲓⲥ

ⲛⲧⲥⲱϣⲉ ⲥⲉⲛⲁϫⲟⲟⲥ ϫⲉ ⲕⲉ ⲧⲛⲥⲱϣⲉ

4 ⲉⲃⲟⲗ ⲛⲁⲛ ⲛⲧⲟⲟⲧ ⲥⲉⲕⲁⲕ ⲁϩⲏⲧ ⲙⲡⲟⲧⲙ

ⲧⲟ ⲉⲃⲟⲗ ⲉⲧⲟⲧⲕⲁⲁⲥ ⲉⲃⲟⲗ ⲛⲁⲧ ⲛⲥⲉϯ ⲧⲟⲧ

6 ⲥⲱϣⲉ ⲛⲁⲧ ⲇⲓⲁ ⲧⲟⲧⲧⲟ ϯϫⲱ ⲙⲙⲟⲥ ϫⲉ ⲉϥ·

ϣⲁⲉⲓⲙⲉ ⲛϭⲓ ⲡϫⲉⲉ[.] ⲛⲏⲉⲓ ϫⲉ ϥⲛⲏⲧ ⲛϭⲓ

8 ⲡⲣⲉϥϫⲓⲟⲧⲉ ϥⲛⲁⲣⲟⲉⲓⲥ ⲉⲙⲡⲁⲧⲉϥ·ⲉⲓ ⲛϥⲧⲙ

ⲕⲁⲁϥ· ⲉϣⲟϫⲧ· ⲉϩⲟⲧⲛ ⲉⲡⲉϥⲏⲉⲓ ⲛⲧⲉ ⲧⲉϥ·

10 ⲙⲛⲧⲉⲣⲟ ⲉⲧⲣⲉϥϥⲓ ⲛⲛⲉϥ·ⲥⲕⲉⲧⲟⲥ ⲛⲧⲱⲧⲛ

29 ⲥⲟⲃⲕ *sic; l.* ⲉⲥⲥⲟⲃⲕ

33 ⲛϩⲁⲗⲁⲧⲉ *sic; l.* ⲛⲛϩⲁⲗⲁⲧⲉ

3 and 5 For ⲕⲱ ⲉⲃⲟⲗ ⲛⲁ″ with same expression for a piece of land as object, *cf.* Ryl 151,2; 159,18

7 ⲡϫⲉⲉ[.] *sic;* either for ⲡϫⲟⲉⲓⲥ or it is an unstressed form as in ⲃⲉ ⲛⲉⲗⲟⲟⲗⲉ 88, 13

14

24 and their leaves do not fall.
Whoever knows them will not taste death.

26 (20) The disciples (μαθητής) said to Jesus: Tell
us what the Kingdom of Heaven is

28 like. He said to them: It is like
a mustard-seed, smaller than (παρά)

30 all seeds. But (δέ) when (ὅταν) it
falls on the tilled earth, it

32 produces a large branch and becomes
shelter (σκέπη) for ‹the› birds of heaven.

34 (21) Mary said to Jesus: Whom are thy disciples (μαθητής)
like? He said: They are like

85 little children who have installed themselves in a field

2 which is not theirs. When (ὅταν) the owners of the field come,
they will say: "Release to us our field".

4 They take off their clothes before them
to release it (the field) to them and to give back

6 their field to them. Therefore (διὰ τοῦτο) I say:
If the lord of the house knows that the thief is coming,

8 he will stay awake before he comes and will not
let him dig through into his house of his

10 kingdom to carry away his goods (σκεῦος). You

ⲇⲉ ⲣⲟⲉⲓⲥ ϩⲁⲧⲉϩⲏ ⲙ̄ⲡⲕⲟⲥⲙⲟⲥ ⲙⲟⲧⲣ ⲙ̄

12 ⲙⲱⲧⲛ ⲉⲭⲛ ⲛⲉⲧⲛ̄ϯⲡⲉ ϩⲛⲛ ⲟⲩⲛⲟϭ ⲛⲁⲧ

ⲛⲁⲙⲓⲥ ϣⲓⲛⲁ ⲇⲉ ⲛⲉⲛⲗ̄ⲛⲥⲧⲏⲥ ϩⲉ ⲉϩⲓⲛ ⲉⲉⲓ

14 ϣⲁⲣⲱⲧⲛ ⲉⲡⲉⲓ ⲧⲉⲭⲣⲉⲓⲁ ⲉⲧⲉⲧⲛ̄ϭⲟⲱϣⲧ`

ⲉⲃⲟⲗ ϩⲏⲧⲥ̄ ⲥⲉⲛⲁϩⲉ ⲉⲣⲟⲥ ⲙⲁⲣⲉϥϣⲱⲡⲉ

16 ϩⲛ ⲧⲉⲧⲛⲙⲏⲧⲉ ⲛ̄ϭⲓ ⲟⲩⲣⲱⲙⲉ ⲛⲉⲡⲓⲥⲧⲓ

ⲙⲱⲛ ⲛ̄ⲧⲁⲣⲉⲡⲕⲁⲣⲡⲟⲥ ⲡⲱϩ ⲁϥⲉⲓ ϩⲛⲛ ⲟⲩ

18 ϭⲉⲡⲏ ⲉⲡⲉϥⲁⲥⲟ ϩⲛ ⲧⲉϥϭⲓϫ̄ ⲁϥϩⲁⲥϥ ⲡⲉ

ⲧⲉ ⲟⲩⲛ̄ ⲙⲁⲁϫⲉ ⲙ̄ⲙⲟϥ` ⲉⲥⲱⲧⲙ̄ ⲙⲁⲣⲉϥⲥⲱⲧⲙ̄

20 (22) ⲁⲓⲥ ⲛⲁⲩ ⲁϩⲛ̄ⲕⲟⲧⲉⲓ ⲉⲧϫ̄ⲓ ⲉⲣⲱⲧⲉ ⲡⲉϫⲁϥ ⲛ̄

ⲛⲉϥⲙⲁⲑⲏⲧⲏⲥ ⲇⲉ ⲛⲉⲉⲓⲕⲟⲧⲉⲓ ⲉⲧϫ̄ⲓ ⲉⲣⲱ

22 ⲧⲉ ⲉⲧⲛ̄ⲧⲱⲛ ⲁⲛⲉⲧⲃⲏⲕ` ⲉϩⲟⲩⲛ ⲁⲧⲙ̄ⲛ

ⲧⲉⲣⲟ ⲡⲉϫⲁⲩ ⲛⲁϥ ⲇⲉ ⲉⲉⲓ ⲉⲛⲟ ⲛ̄ⲕⲟⲧⲉⲓ ⲧⲏ

24 ⲛⲁⲃⲱⲕ` ⲉϩⲟⲩⲛ ⲉⲧⲙⲛ̄ⲧⲉⲣⲟ ⲡⲉϫⲉ ⲓⲏⲥ ⲛⲁⲩ

ⲇⲉ ϩⲟⲧⲁⲛ ⲉⲧⲉⲧⲛ̄ϣⲁⲣ ⲡⲥⲛⲁⲩ ⲟⲩⲁ ⲁⲧⲱ ⲉ

26 ⲧⲉⲧⲛ̄ϣⲁⲣ ⲡⲥⲁ ⲛϩⲟⲩⲛ ⲛ̄ⲑⲉ ⲙ̄ⲡⲥⲁ ⲛⲃⲟⲗ

ⲁⲧⲱ ⲡⲥⲁ ⲛⲃⲟⲗ ⲛ̄ⲑⲉ ⲙ̄ⲡⲥⲁ ⲛϩⲟⲩⲛ ⲁⲧⲱ ⲡⲥⲁ

28 ⲧⲡⲉ ⲛ̄ⲑⲉ ⲙ̄ⲡⲥⲁ ⲙⲡⲓⲧⲛ ⲁⲧⲱ ϣⲓⲛⲁ ⲉⲧⲉ

ⲧⲛⲁⲉⲓⲣⲉ ⲙ̄ⲫⲟ`ⲟⲩⲧ` ⲙⲛ ⲧⲥϩⲓⲙⲉ ⲙ̄ⲡⲓⲟⲩⲁ

30 ⲟⲩⲱⲧ ϫⲉⲕⲁⲁⲥ ⲛⲉϥϩⲟⲟⲩⲧ` ⲣ̄ ϩⲟⲟⲩⲧ` ⲛⲧⲉ

ⲧⲥϩⲓⲙⲉ ⲣ̄ ⲥϩⲓⲙⲉ ϩⲟⲧⲁⲛ ⲉⲧⲉⲧⲛ̄ϣⲁⲉⲓⲣⲉ

32 ⲛ̄ϩⲛ̄ⲃⲁⲗ ⲉⲡⲙⲁ ⲛⲟⲩⲃⲁⲗ` ⲁⲧⲱ ⲟⲩϭⲓϫ`

ⲉⲡⲙⲁ ⲛⲛⲟⲩϭⲓϫ` ⲁⲧⲱ ⲟⲩⲉⲣⲏⲧⲉ ⲉⲡⲙⲁ

34 ⲛⲟⲩⲉⲣⲏⲧⲉ ⲟⲩϩⲓⲕⲱⲛ` ⲉⲡⲙⲁ ⲛⲟⲩϩⲓⲕⲱ

18 ϩⲁⲥϥ for classical Sahidic ⲟϩⲥϥ

23 ⲉⲉⲓ ⲉⲛⲟ for ⲉⲉⲓⲉ ⲉⲛⲟ (haplography)

33 and 34 ⲟⲩⲉⲣⲏⲧⲉ for ⲟⲩⲟⲩⲉⲣⲏⲧⲉ

then (δέ) must watch for the world (κόσμος), gird

12 up your loins with great strength (δύναμις)

lest (ἵνα) the brigands (λῃστής) find (a) way to come

14 to you, because (ἐπεί) they will find the advantage (χρεία)

which you expect. Let there be

16 among you a man of understanding (ἐπιστήμων);

when the fruit (καρπός) ripened, he came quickly

18 with his sickle in his hand, he reaped it.

Whoever has ears to hear let him hear.

20 (22) Jesus saw children who were being suckled. He said to

his disciples (μαθητής): These children who are being suckled

22 are like those who enter the Kingdom.

They said to Him: Shall we then, being children,

24 enter the Kingdom? Jesus said to them:

When (ὅταν) you make the two one, and

26 when you make the inner as the outer

and the outer as the inner and the above

28 as the below, and when (ἵνα)

you make the male and the female into a single one,

30 so that the male will not be male and

the female (not) be female, when (ὅταν) you make

32 eyes in the place of an eye, and a hand

in the place of a hand, and a foot in the place

34 of a foot, (and) an image (εἰκών) in the place of an image (εἰκών),

ⲧⲟⲧⲉ ⲧⲉⲧⲛⲁⲃⲱⲕ` ⲉϩⲟⲩⲛ [ⲉⲧⲙⲛⲧⲉⲣⲟ]

86 (23) ⲡⲉϫⲉ ⲓⲥ ϫⲉ ϯⲛⲁⲥⲉⲧⲡ ⲧⲏⲛⲉ ⲟⲩⲁ ⲉⲃⲟⲗ

2 ϩⲛ ϣⲟ ⲁⲩⲱ ⲥⲛⲁⲩ ⲉⲃⲟⲗ ϩⲛ ⲧⲃⲁ ⲁⲩⲱ
ⲥⲉⲛⲁϣⲉ ⲉⲣⲁⲧⲟⲩ ⲉⲩⲟ ⲟⲩⲁ ⲟⲩⲱⲧ` (24) ⲡⲉ

4 ϫⲉ ⲛⲉϥⲙⲁⲑⲏⲧⲏⲥ ϫⲉ ⲙⲁⲧⲥⲉⲃⲟⲛ` ⲉⲡⲧⲟ
ⲡⲟⲥ ⲉⲧⲕⲙⲙⲁⲩ ⲉⲡⲉⲓ ⲧⲁⲛⲁⲅⲕⲏ ⲉⲣⲟⲛ ⲧⲉ

6 ⲉⲧⲣⲛϣⲓⲛⲉ ⲛⲥⲱϥ` ⲡⲉϫⲁϥ` ⲛⲁⲩ ϫⲉ ⲡⲉⲧⲉⲩ
ⲛ ⲙⲁⲁϫⲉ ⲙⲙⲟϥ ⲙⲁⲣⲉϥ`ⲥⲱⲧⲙ ⲟⲩⲛ ⲟⲩ

8 ⲟⲉⲓⲛ` ϣⲟⲟⲡ ⲙⲫⲟⲩⲛ ⲛⲛⲟⲩⲣⲙⲟⲩⲟⲉⲓⲛ
ⲁⲩⲱ ϥⲣ ⲟⲩⲟⲉⲓⲛ ⲉⲡⲕⲟⲥⲙⲟⲥ ⲧⲏⲣϥ` ⲉϥⲧⲙ

10 ⲣ ⲟⲩⲟⲉⲓⲛ· ⲟⲩⲕⲁⲕⲉ ⲡⲉ (25) ⲡⲉϫⲉ ⲓⲥ ϫⲉ ⲙⲉⲣⲉ
ⲡⲉⲕⲥⲟⲛ ⲛⲑⲉ ⲛⲧⲉⲕ`ⲯⲩⲭⲏ ⲉⲣⲓⲧⲏⲣⲉⲓ ⲙⲙⲟϥ

12 ⲛⲑⲉ ⲛⲧⲉⲗⲟⲩ ⲙⲡⲉⲕ`ⲃⲁⲗ` (26) ⲡⲉϫⲉ ⲓⲥ ϫⲉ ⲡϫⲏ
ⲉⲧϩⲙ ⲡⲃⲁⲗ ⲙⲡⲉⲕⲥⲟⲛ ⲕⲛⲁⲩ ⲉⲣⲟϥ` ⲡⲥⲟⲉⲓ

14 ϫⲉ ⲉⲧϩⲙ ⲡⲉⲕⲃⲁⲗ ⲕⲛⲁⲩ ⲁⲛ ⲉⲣⲟϥ` ϩⲟⲧⲁⲛ
ⲉⲕϣⲁⲛⲛⲟⲩϫⲉ ⲙⲡⲥⲟⲉⲓ ⲉⲃⲟⲗ ϩⲙ ⲡⲉⲕ`

16 ⲃⲁⲗ ⲧⲟⲧⲉ ⲕⲛⲁⲛⲁⲩ ⲉⲃⲟⲗ ⲉⲛⲟⲩϫⲉ ⲙⲡϫⲏ
ⲉⲃⲟⲗ ϩⲙ ⲡⲃⲁⲗ ⲙⲡⲉⲕⲥⲟⲛ (27) ⲉⲧⲉⲧⲙⲣⲛⲏ

18 ⲥⲧⲉⲩⲉ ⲉⲡⲕⲟⲥⲙⲟⲥ ⲧⲉⲧⲛⲁϩⲉ ⲁⲛ ⲉⲧⲙⲛⲧⲉ
ⲣⲟ ⲉⲧⲉⲧⲛⲧⲙⲉⲓⲣⲉ ⲙⲡⲥⲁⲙⲃⲁⲧⲟⲛ ⲛⲥⲁⲃ`

20 ⲃⲁⲧⲟⲛ ⲛⲧⲉⲧⲛⲁⲛⲁⲩ ⲁⲛ ⲉⲡⲉⲓⲱⲧ` (28) ⲡⲉϫⲉ
ⲓⲥ ϫⲉ ⲁⲉⲓⲱϩⲉ ⲉⲣⲁⲧ· ϩⲛ ⲧⲙⲏⲧⲉ ⲙⲡⲕⲟⲥ

17 ⲉⲧⲉⲧⲙ *sic*; 1. ⲉⲧⲉⲧⲛⲧⲙ.   Before it ⲡⲉϫⲉ ⲓⲥ ϫⲉ is omitted

18

then (τότε) shall you enter [the Kingdom].

86   (23) Jesus said: I shall choose you, one out

2 of a thousand, and two out of ten thousand, and
they shall stand as a single one.

4 (24) His disciples (μαθητής) said: Show us the place (τόπος)
where Thou art, for (ἐπεί) it is necessary (ἀνάγκη) for us

6 to seek it. He said to them: Whoever has
ears let him hear. Within a man of light

8 there is light
and he lights the whole world (κόσμος). When he

10 does not shine, there is darkness. (25) Jesus said: Love
thy brother as thy soul (ψυχή), guard (τηρεῖν) him

12 as the apple of thine eye. (26) Jesus said: The mote
that is in thy brother's eye thou seest,

14 but (δέ) the beam that is in thine eye, thou seest not. When (ὅταν)
thou castest the beam out of thine

16 eye, then (τότε) thou wilt see clearly to cast the mote
out of thy brother's eye. (27) ‹ Jesus said:› If you fast (νηστεύειν) not

18 from the world (κόσμος), you will not find the Kingdom;
if you keep not the Sabbath (σάββατον) as Sabbath (σάββατον),

20 you will not see the Father.

(28) Jesus said: I took my stand in the midst of the world (κόσμος)

---

3 "single one"; same sense as μοναχός in p. 84, 4.
12 "apple"; lit.: "pupil".
19 "keep .. as Sabbath"; lit.: "make into Sabbath", translates: σαββατίζειν.

22 ⲙⲟⲥ ⲁⲩⲱ ⲁⲉⲓⲟⲩⲱⲛϩ ⲉⲃⲟⲗ ⲛⲁⲩ ϩⲛ ⲥⲁⲣⲝ

ⲁⲉⲓϩⲉ ⲉⲣⲟⲟⲩ ⲧⲏⲣⲟⲩ ⲉⲩⲧⲁϩⲉ ⲙ̄ⲡⲓϩⲉ ⲉⲗⲁ

24 ⲁⲩ ⲛ̄ϩⲏⲧⲟⲩ ⲉϥⲟⲃⲉ ⲁⲩⲱ ⲁⲧⲁⲯⲩⲭⲏ ϯ ⲧⲕⲁⲥ

ⲉϫⲛ ⲛ̄ϣⲏⲣⲉ ⲛ̄ⲣⲣⲱⲙⲉ ϫⲉ ϩⲛ̄ⲃⲗ̄ⲗⲉⲉⲩ

26 ⲉ ⲛⲉ ϩⲙ̄ ⲡⲟⲩϩⲏⲧ· ⲁⲩⲱ ⲥⲉⲛⲁⲩ ⲉⲃⲟⲗ ⲁⲛ

ϫⲉ ⲛ̄ⲧⲁⲩⲉⲓ ⲉⲡⲕⲟⲥⲙⲟⲥ ⲉⲩϣⲟⲩⲉⲓⲧ· ⲉⲩ·

28 ϣⲓⲛⲉ ⲟⲛ ⲉⲧⲣⲟⲩⲉⲓ ⲉⲃⲟⲗ ϩⲙ̄ ⲡⲕⲟⲥⲙⲟⲥ

ⲉⲩϣⲟⲩⲉⲓⲧ ⲡⲗⲏⲛ ⲧⲉⲛⲟⲩ ⲥⲉⲧⲟϩⲉ ϩⲟ

30 ⲧⲁⲛ ⲉⲩϣⲁⲛⲛⲉϩ ⲡⲟⲩⲏⲣⲡ· ⲧⲟⲧⲉ ⲥⲉⲛⲁⲣ̄

ⲙⲉⲧⲁⲛⲟⲉⲓ (29) ⲡⲉϫⲉ ⲓ̅ⲥ̅ ⲉⲩϫⲉ ⲛ̄ⲧⲁⲧⲥⲁⲣⲝ·

32 ϣⲱⲡⲉ ⲉⲧⲃⲉ ⲡⲛⲁ ⲟⲩϣⲡⲏⲣⲉ ⲧⲉ ⲉϣ

ϫⲉ ⲡⲛⲁ ⲇⲉ ⲉⲧⲃⲉ ⲡⲥⲱⲙⲁ ⲟⲩϣⲡⲏⲣⲉ

34 ⲛ̄ϣⲡⲏⲣⲉ ⲡⲉ· ⲁⲗⲗⲁ ⲁⲛⲟⲕ· ϯⲣ̄ ϣⲡⲏⲣⲉ

87 ⲙ̄ⲡⲁⲉⲓ ϫⲉ ⲡⲱ[ⲥ ⲧⲉ]ⲉⲓⲛⲟϭ ⲙ̄ⲙⲛ̄ⲧⲣⲙⲙⲁ

2 ⲟ ⲁⲥⲟⲩⲱϩ ϩⲛ ⲧⲉⲉⲓⲙⲛ̄ⲧϩⲏⲕⲉ (30) ⲡⲉϫⲉ ⲓ̅ⲥ̅

ϫⲉ ⲡⲙⲁ ⲉⲩⲛ̄ ϣⲟⲙⲧ ⲛ̄ⲛⲟⲩⲧⲉ ⲙ̄ⲙⲁⲩ ϩⲛ̄

4 ⲛⲟⲩⲧⲉ ⲛⲉ ⲡⲙⲁ ⲉⲩⲛ̄ ⲥⲛⲁⲩ ⲏ ⲟⲩⲁ ⲁⲛⲟⲕ

ϯϣⲟⲟⲡ· ⲛⲙ̄ⲙⲁϥ· (31) ⲡⲉϫⲉ ⲓ̅ⲥ̅ ⲙⲛ̄ ⲡⲣⲟⲫⲏ

6 ⲧⲏⲥ ϣⲏⲡ· ϩⲙ̄ ⲡⲉϥϯⲙⲉ ⲙⲁⲣⲉⲥⲟⲉⲓⲛ ⲣ̄ⲑⲉ

ⲣⲁⲡⲉⲩⲉ ⲛ̄ⲛⲉⲧ·ⲥⲟⲟⲩⲛ ⲙ̄ⲙⲟϥ· (32) ⲡⲉϫⲉ ⲓ̅ⲥ̅

8 ϫⲉ ⲟⲩⲡⲟⲗⲓⲥ ⲉⲩⲕⲱⲧ ⲙ̄ⲙⲟⲥ ϩⲓϫⲛ̄ ⲟⲩⲧⲟ

ⲟⲩ ⲉϥϫⲟⲥⲉ ⲉⲥⲧⲁϫⲣⲏⲩ ⲁⲛ ϭⲟⲙ ⲛ̄ⲥϩⲉ

10 ⲟⲩⲇⲉ ⲥⲛⲁϣ ϩⲱⲡ· ⲁⲛ (33) ⲡⲉϫⲉ ⲓ̅ⲥ̅ ⲡⲉⲧ·ⲕⲛⲁ

ⲥⲱⲧⲙ̄ ⲉⲣⲟϥ ϩⲙ̄ ⲡⲉⲕ·ⲙⲁⲁϫⲉ ϩⲙ̄ ⲡⲕⲉⲙⲁ

12 ⲁϫⲉ ⲧⲁϣⲉⲟⲉⲓϣ· ⲙ̄ⲙⲟϥ ϩⲓϫⲛ̄ ⲛⲉⲧⲛ̄ϫⲉ

32 and 33 ⲡⲛⲁ *sic*; *l.* ⲡⲡⲛⲁ

34 ⲡⲉ *sic*; *l.* ⲧⲉ

22 and in flesh (σάρξ) I appeared to them;
I found them all drunk, I found none

24 among them athirst. And my soul (ψυχή) was afflicted
for the sons of men, because they are blind

26 in their heart and do not see
that empty they have come into the world (κόσμος)

28 (and that) empty they seek to go out of the world (κόσμος) again.
But (πλήν) now they are drunk.

30 When (ὅταν) they have shaken off their wine, then (τότε) will **they**
repent (μετανοεῖν). (29) Jesus said: If the flesh (σάρξ)

32 has come into existence because of ‹the› spirit (πνεῦμα), it is a marvel;
but (δέ) if ‹the› spirit (πνεῦμα) (has come into existence) because of

34 it is a marvel of marvels. But (ἀλλά) I marvel   [the body (σῶμα),

87   at how (πῶς) this great wealth

2 has made its home in this poverty. (30) Jesus said:
Where there are three gods,

4 they are gods; where there are two or (ἤ) one, I
am with him. (31) Jesus said: No prophet (προφήτης)

6 is acceptable in his village, no physician heals (θεραπεύειν)
those who know him. (32) Jesus said:

8 A city (πόλις) being built on a high mountain
(and) fortified can not fall

10 nor (οὐδέ) can it (ever) be hidden. (33) Jesus said: What thou shalt
hear in thine ear (and) in the other ear,

12 that preach from your housetops;

27 "that", or "because".

ⲙⲡⲱⲣ ⲙⲁⲣⲉⲗⲁⲁⲩ˙ ⲅⲁⲣ ϫⲉⲣⲉ ϩⲏⲃⲥ ⲛ̄ϥ˙

14 ⲕⲁⲁϥ˙ ϩⲁ ⲙⲁⲁϫⲉ ⲟⲩⲇⲉ ⲙⲁϥⲕⲁⲁϥ˙ ϩⲙ̄ ⲙⲁ
ⲉϥϩⲏⲡ˙ ⲁⲗⲗⲁ ⲉϣⲁⲣⲉϥⲕⲁⲁϥ ϩⲓϫⲛ̄ ⲧⲗⲩ

16 ⲭⲛⲓⲁ ϫⲉⲕⲁⲁⲥ ⲟⲩⲟⲛ ⲛⲓⲙ˙ ⲉⲧⲃⲏⲕ˙ ⲉϩⲟⲩⲛ
ⲁⲩⲱ ⲉⲧⲛⲏⲩ ⲉⲃⲟⲗ ⲉⲩⲛⲁⲛⲁⲩ ⲁⲡⲉϥⲟⲩ

18 ⲟⲉⲓⲛ (34) ⲡⲉϫⲉ ⲓ̄ⲥ̄ ϫⲉ ⲟⲩⲃⲗ̄ⲗⲉ ⲉϥϣⲁⲛⲥⲱⲕ
ϩⲏⲧϥ˙ ⲛ̄ⲛⲟⲩⲃⲗ̄ⲗⲉ ϣⲁⲩϩⲉ ⲙ̄ⲡⲉⲥⲛⲁⲩ

20 ⲉⲡⲉⲥⲏⲧ˙ ⲉⲩϩⲓⲉⲓⲧ˙ (35) ⲡⲉϫⲉ ⲓ̄ⲥ̄ ⲙⲛ̄ ϭⲟⲙ
ⲛ̄ⲧⲉⲟⲩⲁ ⲃⲱⲕ˙ ⲉϩⲟⲩⲛ ⲉⲡⲏⲉⲓ ⲙ̄ⲡϫⲱ

22 ⲱⲣⲉ ⲛ̄ϥϫⲓⲧϥ˙ ⲛ̄ϫⲛⲁϩ ⲉⲓⲙⲏⲧⲓ ⲛ̄ϥⲙⲟⲩⲣ
ⲛ̄ⲛⲉϥϭⲓϫ˙ ⲧⲟⲧⲉ ϥⲛⲁⲡⲱⲛⲉ ⲉⲃⲟⲗ

24 ⲙ̄ⲡⲉϥⲏⲉⲓ (36) ⲡⲉϫⲉ ⲓ̄ⲥ̄ ⲙⲛ̄ϥⲓ ⲣⲟⲟⲩϣ ϫⲓ
ϩⲧⲟⲟⲧⲉ ϣⲁ ⲣⲟⲩϩⲉ ⲁⲩⲱ ϫⲓⲛ ϩⲓⲣⲟⲩϩⲉ

26 ϣⲁ ϩⲧⲟⲟⲩⲉ ϫⲉ ⲟⲩ ⲡⲉ ⲉⲧⲛⲁⲧⲁⲁϥ ϩⲓⲱⲧ˙
ⲧⲏⲩⲧⲛ̄ (37) ⲡⲉϫⲉ ⲛⲉϥⲙⲁⲑⲏⲧⲏⲥ ϫⲉ ⲁϣ ⲛ̄

28 ϩⲟⲟⲩ ⲉⲕⲛⲁⲟⲩⲱⲛϩ ⲉⲃⲟⲗ ⲛⲁⲛ ⲁⲩⲱ ⲁϣ
ⲛ̄ϩⲟⲟⲩ ⲉⲛⲁⲛⲁⲩ ⲉⲣⲟⲕ˙ ⲡⲉϫⲉ ⲓ̄ⲥ̄ ϫⲉ ϩⲟ

30 ⲧⲁⲛ ⲉⲧⲉⲧⲛ̄ϣⲁⲕⲉⲕ ⲧⲏⲩⲧⲛ̄ ⲉϩⲏⲩ ⲙ̄ⲡⲉ
ⲧⲛ̄ϣⲓⲡⲉ ⲁⲩⲱ ⲛ̄ⲧⲉⲧⲛ̄ϥⲓ ⲛ̄ⲛⲉⲧⲛ̄ϣⲧⲏⲛ

32 ⲛ̄ⲧⲉⲧⲛ̄ⲕⲁⲁⲩ ϩⲁ ⲡⲉⲥⲛⲧ˙ ⲛ̄ⲛⲉⲧⲛ̄ⲟⲩⲉⲣⲏ
ⲧⲉ ⲛ̄ⲑⲉ ⲛ̄ⲛⲓⲕⲟⲩⲉⲓ ⲛ̄ϣⲏⲣⲉ ϣⲏⲙ˙ ⲛ̄ⲧⲉ

34 ⲧⲛ̄ϫⲟⲡϫⲡ̄ ⲙ̄ⲙⲟⲟⲩ ⲧⲟⲧ[ⲉ ⲧⲉⲧⲛⲁⲛⲁⲩ

88 ⲁ ⲡϣⲏⲣⲉ ⲙ̄ⲡⲉⲧⲟⲛϩ ⲁⲩⲱ ⲧⲉⲧⲛⲁⲣ̄

2 ϩⲟⲧⲉ ⲁⲛ (38) ⲡⲉϫⲉ ⲓ̄ⲥ̄ ϫⲉ ϩⲁϩ ⲛ̄ⲥⲟⲡ ⲁⲧⲉⲧⲛ̄
ⲣⲉⲡⲓⲑⲩⲙⲉⲓ ⲉⲥⲱⲧⲙ̄ ⲁⲛⲉⲉⲓϣⲁϫⲉ ⲛⲁⲉⲓ

4 ⲉϯϫⲱ ⲙ̄ⲙⲟⲟⲩ ⲛⲏⲧⲛ̄ ⲁⲩⲱ ⲙⲛ̄ⲧⲏⲧⲛ̄

30/31 ⲙ̄ⲡⲉⲧⲛ̄ for ⲉⲙⲡⲉⲧⲛ̄ (?)

for (γάρ) no one lights a lamp and

14 puts it under a bushel, nor (οὐδέ) does he put it in a
hidden place, but (ἀλλά) he sets it on the lampstand (λυχνία),

16 so that all who come in
and go out may see its light.

18 (34) Jesus said: If a blind man leads
a blind man, both of them fall

20 into a pit. (35) Jesus said: It is not possible
for one to enter the house of the strong (man)

22 and take him (or: it) by force unless (εἰ μή τι) he bind
his hands; then (τότε) will he ransack his house.

24 (36) Jesus said: Take no thought from
morning until evening and from evening

26 until morning for what you shall put on.
(37) His disciples (μαθητής) said: When

28 wilt Thou be revealed to us and when
will we see Thee? Jesus said: When (ὅταν)

30 you take off your clothing without
being ashamed, and take your clothes

32 and put them under your feet
as the little children and

34 tread on them, then (τότε) [shall you behold]

88 the Son of the Living (One) and you shall not fear.

2 (38) Jesus said: Many times have you
desired (ἐπιθυμεῖν) to hear these words

4 which I say to you, and you have

30/31 Or: "when you take off your shame".

ⲕⲉⲟⲩⲁ ⲉⲥⲟⲧⲙⲟⲩ ⲛ̄ⲧⲟⲟⲧϥ ⲟⲩⲛ̄ ⲟ̄ⲏⲟⲟ

6 ⲟⲩ ⲛⲁϣⲱⲡⲉ ⲛ̄ⲧⲉⲧⲛ̄ϣⲓⲛⲉ ⲛ̄ⲥⲱⲉⲓ ⲧⲉ

ⲧⲛ̄ⲁϩⲉ ⲁⲛ' ⲉⲣⲟⲉⲓ' (39) ⲡⲉⲝⲉ ⲓ̄ⲥ̄ ⲝⲉ ⲙ̄ⲫⲁⲣⲓⲥⲁⲓ

8 ⲟⲥ ⲙⲛ̄ ⲛ̄ⲅⲣⲁⲙⲙⲁⲧⲉⲩⲥ ⲁⲩϫⲓ ⲛ̄ϣⲁϣⲧ'

ⲛ̄ⲧⲅⲛ̄ⲱⲥⲓⲥ ⲁⲩϩⲟⲡⲟⲩ ⲟⲩⲧⲉ ⲙ̄ⲡⲟⲩⲃⲱⲕ

10 ⲉϩⲟⲩⲛ ⲁⲩⲱ ⲛⲉⲧⲟⲩⲱϣ ⲉⲃⲱⲕ' ⲉϩⲟⲩⲛ ⲙ̄

ⲡⲟⲩⲕⲁⲁⲩ ⲛ̄ⲧⲱⲧⲛ̄ ⲇⲉ ϣⲱⲡⲉ ⲙ̄ⲫⲣⲟⲛⲓⲙⲟⲥ

12 ⲛ̄ⲑⲉ ⲛ̄ⲛ̄ϩⲟϥ' ⲁⲩⲱ ⲛ̄ⲁⲕⲉⲣⲁⲓⲟⲥ ⲛ̄ⲑⲉ ⲛ̄ⲛ̄

ϭⲣⲟⲙ'ⲡⲉ (40) ⲡⲉⲝⲉ ⲓ̄ⲥ̄ ⲟⲩⲃⲉ ⲛⲉⲗⲟⲟⲗⲉ ⲁⲩ

14 ⲧⲟϭⲥ ⲙ̄ⲡⲥⲁ ⲛ̄ⲃⲟⲗ ⲙ̄ⲡⲉⲓⲱⲧ' ⲁⲩⲱ ⲉⲥⲧⲁ

ⲝⲣⲏⲩ ⲁⲛ ⲥⲉⲛⲁⲡⲟⲣⲕⲥ̄ ϩⲁ ⲧⲉⲥⲛⲟⲩⲛⲉ ⲛ̄ⲥ

16 ⲧⲁⲕⲟ (41) ⲡⲉⲝⲉ ⲓ̄ⲥ̄ ⲝⲉ ⲡⲉⲧⲉⲩⲛ̄ⲧⲁϥ ϩⲛ̄ ⲧⲉϥ'

ϭⲓⲝ ⲥⲉⲛⲁϯ ⲛⲁϥ' ⲁⲩⲱ ⲡⲉⲧⲉ ⲙⲛ̄ⲧⲁϥ ⲡⲕⲉ

18 ϣⲏⲙ ⲉⲧⲟⲩⲛ̄ⲧⲁϥ' ⲥⲉⲛⲁϥⲓⲧϥ̄ ⲛ̄ⲧⲟⲟⲧϥ'

(42) ⲡⲉⲝⲉ ⲓ̄ⲥ̄ ⲝⲉ ϣⲱⲡⲉ ⲉⲧⲉⲧⲛ̄ⲣ̄ⲡⲁⲣⲁⲅⲉ

20 (43) ⲡⲉⲝⲁⲩ ⲛⲁϥ' ⲛ̄ϭⲓ ⲛⲉϥ'ⲙⲁⲑⲏⲧⲏⲥ ⲝⲉ ⲛ̄ⲧⲁⲕ

ⲛⲓⲙ' ⲉⲕϫⲱ ⲛ̄ⲛⲁⲓ̈ ⲛⲁⲛ' ϩⲛ̄ ⲛⲉⲧϫⲱ ⲙ̄

22 ⲙⲟⲟⲩ ⲛⲏⲧⲛ̄ ⲛ̄ⲧⲉⲧⲛ̄ⲉⲓⲙⲉ ⲁⲛ ⲝⲉ ⲁⲛⲟⲕ'

ⲛⲓⲙ ⲁⲗⲗⲁ ⲛ̄ⲧⲱⲧⲛ̄ ⲁⲧⲉⲧⲛ̄ϣⲱⲡⲉ ⲛ̄ⲑⲉ ⲛ̄

24 ⲛ̄ⲓ̈ⲟⲩⲇⲁⲓⲟⲥ ⲝⲉ ⲥⲉⲙⲉ ⲙ̄ⲡϣⲏⲛ ⲥⲉⲙⲟⲥ

ⲧⲉ ⲙ̄ⲡⲉϥⲕⲁⲣⲡⲟⲥ ⲁⲩⲱ ⲥⲉⲙⲉ ⲙ̄ⲡⲕⲁⲣⲡⲟⲥ

26 ⲥⲉⲙⲟⲥⲧⲉ ⲙ̄ⲡϣⲏⲛ (44) ⲡⲉⲝⲉ ⲓ̄ⲥ̄ ⲝⲉ ⲡⲉⲧⲁⲝⲉ

ⲟⲩⲁ ⲁⲡⲉⲓⲱⲧ' ⲥⲉⲛⲁⲕⲱ ⲉⲃⲟⲗ ⲛⲁϥ' ⲁⲩⲱ

28 ⲡⲉⲧⲁⲝⲉ ⲟⲩⲁ ⲉⲡϣⲏⲣⲉ ⲥⲉⲛⲁⲕⲱ ⲉⲃⲟⲗ

ⲛⲁϥ' ⲡⲉⲧⲁⲝⲉ ⲟⲩⲁ ⲇⲉ ⲁⲡⲡⲛ̄ⲁ ⲉⲧⲟⲩⲁⲁⲃ

21 ⲡⲉⲝⲉ ⲓ̄ⲥ̄ ⲛⲁⲩ ⲝⲉ is omitted before ϩⲛ

24

no other from whom to hear them. There will be days
6 when you will seek Me (and)
you will not find Me. (39) Jesus said: The Pharisees (Φαρισαῖος)
8 and the Scribes (γραμματεύς) have received the keys
of Knowledge (γνῶσις), they have hidden them. They did not (οὔτε)
10 and they did not let those (enter) who wished.   [enter,
But (δέ) you, become wise (φρόνιμος)
12 as serpents and innocent (ἀκέραιος) as
doves. (40) Jesus said: A vine has been
14 planted without the Father and, as it is not
established, it will be pulled up by its roots and be
16 destroyed. (41) Jesus said: Whoever has in his
hand, to him shall be given; and whoever does not have,
18 from him shall be taken even the little which he has.
(42) Jesus said: Become passers-by (παράγειν).
20 (43) His disciples (μαθητής) said to Him:
Who art Thou that Thou should say these things to us. ‹ Jesus said to
                                        them›: From what I say
22 to you, you do not know who I am,
but (ἀλλά) you have become as
24 the Jews (Ἰουδαῖος), for they love the tree, they hate
its fruit (καρπός) and they love the fruit (καρπός),
26 they hate the tree. (44) Jesus said: Whoever
blasphemes against the Father, it shall be forgiven him, and
28 whoever blasphemes against the Son, it shall be forgiven him;
but (δέ) whoever blasphemes against the Holy Ghost (πνεῦμα),

30 сенакω ан евоⳗ нач· оⲩте ⲟ̄м пⲕаϩ
   оⲩте ϩ̄н тпе (45) пеϫе ⲓ̄ⲥ маⲩϫеⳗе еⳗоо

32 ⳗе евоⳗ ϩ̄н ϣонте оⲩте маⲩⲕωтⳇ·
   ⲕⲛте евоⳗ ϩ̄н ⲥⲣ̄ϭамоⲩⳗ· маⲩ† ⲕарпоⲥ

34 ⲉ[ар оⲩаⲅ]аѳоⲥ ⲣ̄рωме ϣачеıне ⲛ̄
89 оⲩаⲅаѳон евоⳗ ϩ[м̄] печеϩо оⲩⲕа[ⲕоⲥ]

2 ⲣ̄рωме ϣачеıне ⲛ̄ϩⲛ̄пониⲣон евоⳗ
   ϩ̄м печеϩо еѳооⲩ етϩ̄н пеⳅϩⲏⲧ· аⲩ

4 ω ⲛ̄ч̄ϫω ⲛ̄ϩⲛ̄пониⲣон евоⳗ ⲅар ϩ̄м
   ⲫоⲩо ⲙ̄ⲫⲏⲧ· ϣач̄еıне евоⳗ ⲛ̄ϩⲛ̄по

6 ниⲣон (46) пеϫе ⲓ̄ⲥ ϫе ϫıн· аⳡам ϣа ⲓ̄ω̄ϩа
   нⲛⲏⲥ пваптıⲥⲧⲏⲥ ϩ̄н ⲛ̄ϫⲡо ⲛ̄ϩı̄оⲩⲙⲉ

8 ⲙ̄н петϫоⲥⲉ ӓıωϩⲁⲛⲛⲏⲥ пваптı
   ⲥⲧⲏⲥ ϣıна ϫе ноⲩωϣⲡ· ⲛ̄ϭı нечваⳗ

10 аеıϫооⲥ ⳳⲉ ϫе петнашⲱⲡⲉ ϩ̄н тⲏⲩ
   тⲏ еⳅϥ̄о ⲛ̄ⲕоⲩⲉı чнаⲥоⲩωⲛ ⲧⲙ̄ⲛⲧⲉ

12 ро аⲩω ⳅⲛаϫıⲥⲉ ӓıωϩⲁⲛⲛⲏⲥ (47) пеϫе ⲓ̄ⲥ
   ϫе ⲙ̄н ϭом ⲛ̄теоⲩⲣ̄ⲣωⲙⲉ тⲉⳗо аϩⲧⲟ

14 ⲥⲛаⲩ ⲛ̄ⳅϥ̄ϫωⳗⲕ· ⲙ̄пıте ⲥⲛ̄ⲧⲉ аⲩω ⲙ̄н
   ϭом· ⲛ̄теоⲩϩⲙ̄ϩⲁⳗ ϣⲙ̄ϣⲉ ϫоеıⲥ ⲥⲛаⲩ

16 ⲏ ⳅϥ̄ⲛартıма ⲙ̄поⲩа· аⲩω пⲕеоⲩа ⳅϥ̄на
   ⲣ̄оⲩвⲣıⳅⲉ ⲙ̄ⲙоⳅⳇ· ⲙⲁⲣⲉⲣωⲙⲉ ⲥⲉ ⲣ̄паⲥ

18 аⲩω ⲛ̄теⲩноⲩ ⲛⳅϥ̄·επıⲑⲩⲙⲉı аⲥω ⲏⲣⲡ·
   ⲃ̄ⲃⲣ̄ⲣⲉ аⲩω маⲩноⲩⳉ· ⲏⲣⲡ· ⲃ̄ⲃⲣ̄ⲣⲉ еаⲥ

20 ⲕоⲥ ⲛ̄аⲥ ϫеⲕааⲥ ⲛ̄ноⲩⲡωϩ аⲩω маⲩ
   неϫ· ⲏⲣⲡ· ⲛ̄аⲥ еаⲥⲕоⲥ ⲃ̄ⲃⲣ̄ⲣⲉ ϣıна ϫе

9 ноⲩωϣⲡ *sic*; *l.* ноⲩоⲩωϣⲡ

30 it shall not be forgiven him, either (οὔτε) on earth

or (οὔτε) in heaven. (45) Jesus said: They do not harvest grapes

32 from thorns, nor (οὔτε) do they gather

figs from thistles; [for (γάρ)] they give no fruit (καρπός)

34 [A] good [(ἀγ)]αθός) man brings forth

89   good (ἀγαθόν) out of his treasure, an evil (κα[κός)]

2 man brings forth evil things (πονηρόν) out

of his evil treasure, which is in his heart, and

4 speaks evil things (πονηρόν). For (γάρ) out of

the abundance of the heart he brings forth evil things (πονηρόν).

6 (46) Jesus said: From Adam until John

the Baptist (βαπτιστής) there is among those who are born of women

8 none higher than John the Baptist (βαπτιστής),

so that (ἵνα) his eyes will not be broken.

10 But (δέ) I have said that whoever among you

becomes as a child shall know the Kingdom,

12 and he shall become higher than John. (47) Jesus said:

It is impossible for a man to mount two horses

14 and to stretch two bows, and it is impossible

for a servant to serve two masters,

16 otherwise (ἤ) he will honour (τιμᾶν) the one

and offend (ὑβρίζειν) the other. No man drinks old wine

18 and immediately desires ἐπιθυμεῖν) to drink new wine;

and they do not put new (wine into old wineskins (ἀσκός),

20 lest they burst, and they

do not put old wine into a new wineskin (ἀσκός), lest (ἵνα)

22 ⲛⲉϥⲧⲉⲕⲁϥ' ⲙⲁⲧⲭⲗϭ ⲧⲟⲉⲓⲥ ⲛⲁⲥ ⲁϣⲧⲛ̄
ⲛ̄ϣⲁⲉⲓ ⲉⲡⲉⲓ ⲟⲩⲛ ⲟⲩⲡⲱϣ ⲛⲁϣⲱⲡⲉ

24 (48) ⲡⲉⲭⲉ ⲓ̅ⲥ̅ ⲭⲉ ⲉⲣϣⲁⲥⲛⲁⲩ ⲣ̄ ⲉⲓⲣⲏⲛⲏ ⲙⲛ̄
ⲛⲟⲩⲉⲣⲏⲩ ϩⲙ̄ ⲡⲉⲓⲏⲉⲓ ⲟⲩⲱⲧ' ⲥⲉⲛⲁⲭⲟⲟⲥ

26 ⲙ̄ⲡⲧⲁⲩ ⲭⲉ ⲡⲱⲛⲉ ⲉⲃⲟⲗ ⲁⲩⲱ ϥⲛⲁⲡⲱ
ⲱⲛⲉ (49) ⲡⲉⲭⲉ ⲓ̅ⲥ̅ ⲭⲉ ϩⲉⲛⲙⲁⲕⲁⲣⲓⲟⲥ ⲛⲉ ⲛ

28 ⲙⲟⲛⲁⲭⲟⲥ ⲁⲩⲱ ⲉⲧⲥⲟⲧⲡ' ⲭⲉ ⲧⲉⲧⲛⲁ
ϩⲉ ⲁⲧⲙ̄ⲛⲧⲉⲣⲟ ⲭⲉ ⲛ̄ⲧⲱⲧⲛ ϩⲛⲉⲃⲟⲗ

30 ⲛ̄ϩⲏⲧⲥ ⲡⲁⲗⲓⲛ ⲉⲧⲉⲧⲛⲁⲃⲱⲕ' ⲉⲙⲁⲩ (50) ⲡⲉ
ⲭⲉ ⲓ̅ⲥ̅ ⲭⲉ ⲉⲩϣⲁⲛⲭⲟⲟⲥ ⲛⲏⲧⲛ ⲭⲉ ⲛ̄ⲧⲁ

32 ⲧⲉⲧⲛ̄ϣⲱⲡⲉ ⲉⲃⲟⲗ ⲧⲱⲛ ⲭⲟⲟⲥ ⲛⲁⲩ
ⲭⲉ ⲛ̄ⲧⲁⲛⲉⲓ ⲉⲃⲟⲗ ϩⲙ̄ ⲡⲟⲩⲟⲉⲓⲛ ⲡⲙⲁ

34 ⲉⲛⲧⲁⲡⲟⲩⲟⲉⲓⲛ ϣⲱⲡⲉ ⲙ̄ⲙⲁⲩ ⲉⲃⲟⲗ
ϩⲓⲧⲟⲟⲧϥ' ⲟⲩⲁⲁⲧϥ' ⲁϥⲱϩ[ⲉ ⲉⲣⲁⲧϥ]

90 ⲁⲩⲱ ⲁϥⲟⲩⲱⲛϩ [ⲉⲃ]ⲟⲗ ϩⲛ ⲧⲟⲩϩⲓⲕⲱⲛ ⲉⲩ

2 ϣⲁⲭⲟⲟⲥ ⲛⲏⲧⲛ ⲭⲉ ⲛ̄ⲧⲱⲧⲛ ⲡⲉ ⲭⲟⲟⲥ
ⲭⲉ ⲁⲛⲟⲛ ⲛⲉϥϣⲏⲣⲉ ⲁⲩⲱ ⲁⲛⲟⲛ ⲛ̄ⲥⲱⲧⲡ'

4 ⲙ̄ⲡⲉⲓⲱⲧ' ⲉⲧⲟⲛϩ ⲉⲩϣⲁⲛⲭⲛⲉ ⲧⲏⲩⲧⲛ
ⲭⲉ ⲟⲩ ⲡⲉ ⲡⲙⲁⲉⲓⲛ ⲙ̄ⲡⲉⲧⲛⲉⲓⲱⲧ' ⲉⲧϩⲛ

6 ⲧⲏⲩⲧⲛ ⲭⲟⲟⲥ ⲉⲣⲟⲟⲩ ⲭⲉ ⲟⲩⲕⲓⲙ ⲡⲉ ⲙⲛ̄
ⲟⲩⲁⲛⲁⲡⲁⲩⲥⲓⲥ (51) ⲡⲉⲭⲁⲩ ⲛⲁϥ' ⲛ̄ϭⲓ ⲛⲉϥⲙⲁ

8 ⲑⲏⲧⲏⲥ ⲭⲉ ⲁϣ ⲛ̄ϩⲟⲟⲩ ⲉⲧⲁⲛⲁⲡⲁⲩⲥⲓⲥ ⲛ̄
ⲛⲉⲧⲙⲟⲟⲩⲧ' ⲛⲁϣⲱⲡⲉ ⲁⲩⲱ ⲁϣ ⲛ̄ϩⲟⲟⲩ

10 ⲉⲡⲕⲟⲥⲙⲟⲥ ⲃ̄ⲃ̄ⲣⲣⲉ ⲛⲏⲩ ⲡⲉⲭⲁϥ ⲛⲁⲩ ⲭⲉ
ⲧⲏ ⲉⲧⲉⲧⲛ̄ϭⲱϣⲧ' ⲉⲃⲟⲗ ϩⲏⲧⲥ̄ ⲁⲥⲉⲓ ⲁⲗⲗⲁ

12 ⲛ̄ⲧⲱⲧⲛ ⲧⲉⲧⲛ̄ⲥⲟⲟⲩⲛ ⲁⲛ ⲙ̄ⲙⲟⲥ (52) ⲡⲉⲭⲁⲩ

2 ⲡⲉ *sic*; *l.* ⲛⲓⲙ

28

22 it spoil it. They do not sew an old patch on a new garment,
because (ἐπεί) there would come a rent.

24 (48) Jesus said: If two make peace (εἰρήνη) with
each other in this one house, they shall say

26 to the mountain: "Be moved", and it shall be moved.
(49) Jesus said: Blessed (μακάριος) are the

28 solitary (μοναχός) and elect, for you shall
find the Kingdom; because you come from it,

30 (and) you shall go there again (πάλιν).
(50) Jesus said: If they say to you:

32 "From where have you originated?", say to them:
"We have come from the Light,

34 where the Light has originated through
itself. It [stood]

90 and it revealed itself in their image (εἰκών)".

2 If they say to you: "(Who) are you?", say:
"We are His sons and we are the elect

4 of the Living Father". If they ask you:
"What is the sign of your Father in

6 you?", say to them: "It is a movement and a
rest" (ἀνάπαυσις). (51) His disciples (μαθητής) said to Him:

8 When will the repose (ἀνάπαυσις) of
the dead come about and when

10 will the new world (κόσμος) come? He said to them:
What you expect has come, but (ἀλλά)

12 you know it not.

2 "(Who) are you?"; Ms.: "It is you".

ⲛⲁϥ ⲛϭⲓ ⲛⲉϥⲙⲁⲑⲏⲧⲏⲥ ⲍⲉ ⲍⲟⲩⲧ ⲁϥⲧⲉ

14 ⲙⲡⲣⲟⲫⲏⲧⲏⲥ ⲁⲩϣⲁⲍⲉ ϩⲙ ⲡⲓⲥⲣⲁⲏⲗ·

ⲁⲩⲱ ⲁⲩϣⲁⲍⲉ ⲧⲏⲣⲟⲩ ϩⲣⲁⲓ ⲛϩⲏⲧⲕ· ⲡⲉ

16 ⲍⲁϥ ⲛⲁⲩ ⲍⲉ ⲁⲧⲉⲧⲛⲕⲱ ⲙⲡⲉⲧⲟⲛϩ ⲙⲡⲉ

ⲧⲙⲧⲟ ⲉⲃⲟⲗ ⲁⲩⲱ ⲁⲧⲉⲧⲛϣⲁⲍⲉ ϩⲁ ⲛⲉⲧ

18 ⲙⲟⲟⲩⲧ· (53) ⲡⲉⲍⲁⲩ ⲛⲁϥ ⲛϭⲓ ⲛⲉϥⲙⲁⲑⲏⲧⲏⲥ

ⲍⲉ ⲡⲥⲃⲃⲉ ⲣⲱϥⲉⲗⲉⲓ ⲏ ⲙⲙⲟⲛ ⲡⲉⲍⲁϥ·

20 ⲛⲁⲩ ⲍⲉ ⲛⲉϥⲣⲱϥⲉⲗⲉⲓ ⲛⲉⲡⲟⲩⲉⲓⲱⲧ· ⲛⲁ

ⲍⲡⲟⲟⲩ ⲉⲃⲟⲗ ϩⲛ ⲧⲟⲩⲙⲁⲁⲩ ⲉⲩⲥⲃⲃⲏⲩⲧ

22 ⲁⲗⲗⲁ ⲡⲥⲃⲃⲉ ⲙⲙⲉ ϩⲙ ⲡⲛⲁ ⲁϥϭⲛ ϩⲏⲩ

ⲧⲏⲣϥ· (54) ⲡⲉⲍⲉ ⲓⲥ ⲍⲉ ϩⲛⲙⲁⲕⲁⲣⲓⲟⲥ ⲛⲉ ⲛϩⲏ

24 ⲕⲉ ⲍⲉ ⲧⲱⲧⲛ ⲧⲉ ⲧⲙⲛⲧⲉⲣⲟ ⲛⲙⲡⲏⲩⲉ·

(55) ⲡⲉⲍⲉ ⲓⲥ ⲍⲉ ⲡⲉⲧⲁⲙⲉⲥⲧⲉ ⲡⲉϥⲉⲓⲱⲧ·

26 ⲁⲛ· ⲙⲛ ⲧⲉϥⲙⲁⲁⲩ ϥⲛⲁϣ ⲣ ⲙⲁⲑⲏⲧⲏⲥ ⲁⲛ

ⲛⲁⲉⲓ ⲁⲩⲱ ⲛϥⲙⲉⲥⲧⲉ ⲛⲉϥⲥⲛⲏⲩ ⲙⲛ

28 ⲛⲉϥⲥⲱⲛⲉ ⲛϥϥⲓ ⲙⲡⲉϥⲥⳁⲣⲟⲥ ⲛⲧⲁϩⲉ

ϥⲛⲁϣⲱⲡⲉ ⲁⲛ ⲉϥⲟ ⲛⲁⲝⲓⲟⲥ ⲛⲁⲉⲓ (56) ⲡⲉ

30 ⲍⲉ ⲓⲥ ⲍⲉ ⲡⲉⲧⲁϩⲥⲟⲩⲱⲛ ⲡⲕⲟⲥⲙⲟⲥ ⲁϥ·

ϩⲉ ⲉⲩⲡⲧⲱⲙⲁ ⲁⲩⲱ ⲡⲉⲛⲧⲁϩϩⲉ ⲉⲁⲡⲧⲱ

32 ⲙⲁ ⲡⲕⲟⲥⲙⲟⲥ ⲙⲡϣⲁ ⲙⲙⲟϥ ⲁⲛ (57) ⲡⲉ

ⲍⲉ ⲓⲥ ⲍⲉ ⲧⲙⲛⲧⲉⲣⲟ ⲙⲡⲉⲓⲱⲧ· ⲉⲥⲧⲛⲧⲱ

34 ⲁⲩⲣⲱⲙⲉ ⲉⲩⲛⲧⲁϥ ⲙⲙⲁⲩ ⲛⲛⲟⲩϭⲣⲟϭ

[ⲉⲛⲁⲛⲟⲩ]ϥ· ⲁⲡⲉϥⲍⲁⲍⲉ ⲉⲓ ⲛⲧⲟⲩϣⲏ·

91 ⲁϥⲥⲓⲧⲉ ⲛⲟⲩⲍⲓⲍⲁⲛⲓⲟⲛ ⲙⲛ ⲡⲉϭⲣⲟ[ϭ ⲉ]

31 ⲡⲉⲛⲧⲁϩϩⲉ: the second ϩ is added above the line
31 ⲉⲁⲡⲧⲱ *sic*; *l.* ⲉⲩⲡⲧⲱ

(52) His disciples (μαθητής) said to Him: Twenty-four

14 prophets (προφήτης) spoke in Israel

and they all spoke about (lit.: in) Thee.

16 He said to them: You have dismissed the Living (One)

who is before you and you have spoken about the

18 dead. (53) His disciples (μαθητής) said to Him:

Is circumcision profitable (ὠφελεῖν) or (ἤ) not? He said

20 to them: If it were profitable (ὠφελεῖν), their father

would beget them circumcised from their mother.

22 But (ἀλλά) the true circumcision in Spirit (πνεῦμα) has

become profitable in every way. (54) Jesus said: Blessed (μακάριος)

24 for yours is the Kingdom of Heaven.   [are the poor,

(55) Jesus said: Whoever does not hate his father

26 and his mother will not be able to be a disciple (μαθητής) to Me,

and (whoever does not) hate his brethren and

28 his sisters and (does not) take up his cross (σταυρός) in My way

will not be worthy (ἄξιος) of Me.

30 (56) Jesus said: Whoever has known the world (κόσμος) has found

a corpse (πτῶμα), and whoever has found a corpse (πτῶμα),

32 of him the world (κόσμος) is not worthy.

(57) Jesus said: The Kingdom of the Father is like

34 a man who had [good] seed.

His enemy came by night,

91   he sowed a weed (ζιζάνιον) among the good seed.

2 ⲧⲛⲁⲛⲟⲩϥ· ⲙ̄ⲡⲉⲡⲣⲱⲙⲉ ⲕⲟⲟⲧ ⲉϥⲱⲗⲉ

ⲙ̄ⲡϫ̄ϫⲁⲛⲓⲟⲛ ⲡⲉϫⲁϥ ⲛⲁⲩ ϫⲉ ⲙⲏⲡⲱⲥ

4 ⲛ̄ⲧⲉⲧⲛ̄ⲃⲱⲕ ϫⲉ ⲉⲛⲁϩⲱⲗⲉ ⲙ̄ⲡϫ̄ϫⲁⲛⲓⲟ

ⲛ̄ⲧⲉⲧⲛ̄ϩⲱⲗⲉ ⲙ̄ⲡⲥⲟⲟⲧⲟ ⲛ̄ⲙ̄ⲙⲁϥ· ϩⲙ̄ ⲫⲟ

6 ⲟⲩ ⲅⲁⲣ ⲙ̄ⲡⲱϩⲥ̄ ⲛ̄ϫ̄ϫⲁⲛⲓⲟⲛ ⲛⲁⲟⲩⲱⲛϩ

ⲉⲃⲟⲗ· ⲥⲉϩⲟⲗⲟⲩ ⲛ̄ⲥⲉⲣⲟⲕϩⲟⲩ (58) ⲡⲉϫⲉ ⲓⲥ̄

8 ϫⲉ ⲟⲩⲙⲁⲕⲁⲣⲓⲟⲥ ⲡⲉ ⲡⲣⲱⲙⲉ ⲛ̄ⲧⲁϩϩⲓⲥⲉ

ⲁϥϩⲉ ⲁⲡⲱⲛϩ (59) ⲡⲉϫⲉ ⲓⲥ̄ ϫⲉ ϭⲱϣⲧ ⲛ̄ⲥⲁ ⲡⲉ

10 ⲧⲟⲛϩ ϩⲱⲥ ⲉⲧⲉⲧⲛ̄ⲟⲛϩ̄ ϩⲓⲛⲁ ϫⲉ ⲛⲉⲧⲙ̄ⲙⲟⲩ

ⲁⲩⲱ ⲛ̄ⲧⲉⲧⲛ̄ϣⲓⲛⲉ ⲉⲛⲁⲩ ⲉⲣⲟϥ ⲁⲩⲱ ⲧⲉⲧⲛⲁϣ

12 ϭⲙ̄ϭⲟⲙ ⲁⲛ ⲉⲛⲁⲩ (60) ⲁⲩⲥⲁⲙⲁⲣⲉⲓⲧⲏⲥ ⲉϥϥⲓ ⲛ̄

ⲛⲟⲩϩⲓⲉⲓⲃ· ⲉϥⲃⲏⲕ· ⲉϩⲟⲩⲛ ⲉⲧⲟⲩⲇⲁⲓⲁ ⲡⲉ

14 ϫⲁϥ· ⲛ̄ⲛⲉϥ·ⲙⲁⲑⲏⲧⲏⲥ ϫⲉ ⲡⲏ ⲙ̄ⲡⲕⲱⲧⲉ

ⲙ̄ⲡⲉϩⲓⲉⲓⲃ· ⲡⲉϫⲁⲩ ⲛⲁϥ ϫⲉⲕⲁⲁⲥ ⲉϥⲛⲁ

16 ⲙⲟⲟⲩⲧϥ· ⲛ̄ϥⲟⲩⲟⲙϥ· ⲡⲉϫⲁϥ ⲛⲁⲩ ϩⲱⲥ ⲉ

ϥⲟⲛϩ ϥⲛⲁⲟⲩⲟⲙϥ· ⲁⲛ ⲁⲗⲗⲁ ⲉϥϣⲁⲙⲟ

18 ⲟⲩⲧϥ· ⲛ̄ϥϣⲱⲡⲉ ⲛ̄ⲟⲩⲡⲧⲱⲙⲁ ⲡⲉϫⲁⲩ

ϫⲉ ⲛ̄ⲕⲉⲥⲙⲟⲧ ϥⲛⲁϣ ⲁⲥ ⲁⲛ ⲡⲉϫⲁϥ ⲛⲁⲩ

20 ϫⲉ ⲛ̄ⲧⲱⲧⲛ̄ ϩⲱⲧ· ⲧⲏⲩⲧⲛ̄ ϣⲓⲛⲉ ⲛ̄ⲥⲁ ⲟⲩ

ⲧⲟⲡⲟⲥ ⲛⲏⲧⲛ̄ ⲉϩⲟⲩⲛ ⲉⲩⲁⲛⲁⲡⲁⲩⲥⲓⲥ

22 ϫⲉⲕⲁⲁⲥ ⲛ̄ⲛⲉⲧⲛ̄ϣⲱⲡⲉ ⲙ̄ⲡⲧⲱⲙⲁ ⲛ̄ⲥⲉ

ⲟⲩⲱⲙ· ⲧⲏⲩⲧⲛ̄ (61) ⲡⲉϫⲉ ⲓⲥ̄ ⲟⲩⲛ̄ ⲥⲛⲁⲩ ⲛⲁⲙ̄

12 At the beginning of (60) ⲁⲩⲛⲁⲩ is omitted by haplography

32

2 The man did not permit them (the workers) to pull up
the weed (ζιζάνιον). He said to them: Lest perhaps (μήπως)

4 you go to pull up the weed (ζιζάνιον)
and pull up the wheat with it.

6 For (γάρ) on the day of harvest the weeds (ζιζάνιον) will appear,
they (will) pull them and burn them. (58) Jesus said:

8 Blessed (μακάριος) is the man who has suffered,
he has found the Life. (59) Jesus said: Look upon the

10 Living (One) as long as (ὡς) you live, lest (ἵνα) you die
and seek to see Him and be unable

12 to see. (60) ‹They saw› a Samaritan carrying
a lamb on his way to Judea.

14 He said to His disciples (μαθητής): (Why does) this man (carry) the
lamb with him?. They said to Him: In order that he may

16 kill it and eat it. He said to them: As long as (ὡς)
it is alive, he will not eat it, but (ἀλλά) (only) if he has

18 killed it and it has become a corpse (πτῶμα). They said:
Otherwise he will not be able to do it. He said to them:

20 You yourselves, seek a
place (τόπος) for yourselves in Repose (ἀνάπαυσις),

22 lest you become a corpse (πτῶμα) and be eaten.

(61) Jesus said: Two will rest

---

4 "to pull up"; lit.: "saying: "We will pull up".
13 "on his way": lit.: "going".
14-15 lit.: "He concerning (or: around) the lamb". The text must be corrupt.

24 ⲧⲟⲛ ⲙ̄ⲙⲁⲩ ϩⲓ ⲟⲩϭⲗⲟϭ ⲡⲟⲩⲁ ⲛⲁⲙⲟⲩ ⲡⲟⲩ

ⲁ ⲛⲁϣⲏⲣ ⲡⲉϫⲉ ⲥⲁⲗⲱⲙⲏ ⲛ̄ⲧⲁⲕ` ⲛⲓⲙ`

26 ⲡⲣⲱⲙⲉ ϩⲱⲥ ⲉⲃⲟⲗ ϩⲛ̄ ⲟⲩⲁ ⲁⲕⲧⲉ̄ⲗⲟ ⲉϫⲙ̄

ⲡⲁϭⲗⲟϭ ⲁⲩⲱ ⲁⲕ`ⲟⲩⲱⲙ ⲉⲃⲟⲗ ϩⲛ̄ ⲧⲁ

28 ⲧⲣⲁⲡⲉⲍⲁ ⲡⲉϫⲉ ⲓ̄ⲥ̄ ⲛⲁⲥ ϫⲉ ⲁⲛⲟⲕ` ⲡⲉ

ⲡⲉⲧϣⲟⲟⲡ` ⲉⲃⲟⲗ ϩⲙ̄ ⲡⲉⲧϣⲏϣ ⲁⲩⲧ

30 ⲛⲁⲉⲓ ⲉⲃⲟⲗ ϩⲛ̄ ⲛⲁ ⲡⲁⲉⲓⲱⲧ` ⲁⲛⲟⲕ` ⲧⲉⲕ`

ⲙⲁⲑⲏⲧⲏⲥ ⲉⲧⲃⲉ ⲡⲁⲉⲓ ϯϫⲱ ⲙ̄ⲙⲟⲥ ϫⲉ

32 ϩⲟⲧⲁⲛ ⲉϥϣⲁϣⲱⲡⲉ ⲉϥϣⲏϥ` ϥⲛⲁⲙⲟⲩϩ

ⲟⲩⲟⲉⲓⲛ ϩⲟⲧⲁⲛ ⲇⲉ ⲉϥϣⲁⲛϣⲱⲡⲉ ⲉϥ

34 ⲡⲏϣ ϥⲛⲁⲙⲟⲩϩ ⲛ̄ⲕⲁⲕⲉ (62) ⲡⲉϫⲉ [ⲓ̄]ⲥ̄ ϫⲉ ⲉⲓ

ϫⲱ ⲛ̄ⲛⲁⲙⲩⲥⲧⲏⲣⲓⲟⲛ ⲛⲛ[ⲉⲧⲙⲡϣⲁ ⲛ

92   ⲛⲁ]ⲙⲩⲥⲧⲏⲣⲓⲟⲛ ⲡⲉ[ⲧ]ⲉ ⲧⲉⲕⲟⲩⲛⲁⲙ ⲛⲁⲁϥ

2 ⲙ̄ⲛⲧⲣⲉⲧⲉⲕϩⲃⲟⲩⲣ` ⲉⲓⲙⲉ ϫⲉ ⲉⲥⲣ ⲟⲩ (63) ⲡⲉϫⲉ ⲓ̄ⲥ̄

ϫⲉ ⲛⲉⲩⲛ ⲟⲩⲣⲱⲙⲉ ⲙ̄ⲡⲗⲟⲩⲥⲓⲟⲥ ⲉⲩⲛⲧⲁϥ ⲙ̄

4 ⲙⲁⲩ ⲛϩⲁϩ ⲛ̄ⲭⲣⲏⲙⲁ ⲡⲉϫⲁϥ ϫⲉ ϯⲛⲁⲣⲭⲣⲱ ⲛ̄

ⲛⲁⲭⲣⲏⲙⲁ ϫⲉⲕⲁⲁⲥ ⲉⲉⲓⲛⲁϫⲟ ⲛ̄ⲧⲁϣⲥϩ

6 ⲛ̄ⲧⲁⲧⲱϭⲉ ⲛ̄ⲧⲁⲙⲟⲩϩ ⲛ̄ⲛⲁⲉϩⲱⲣ ⲛ̄ⲕⲁⲣ

ⲡⲟⲥ ϣⲓⲛⲁ ϫⲉ ⲛⲓⲣ ϭⲣⲱϩ ⲛ̄ⲗⲁⲁⲩ ⲛⲁⲉⲓ ⲛⲉ

8 ⲛⲉϥⲙⲉⲉⲩⲉ ⲉⲣⲟⲟⲩ ϩⲙ̄ ⲡⲉϥϩⲏⲧ` ⲁⲩⲱ ϩⲛ̄

ⲧⲟⲩϣⲏ ⲉⲧⲙ̄ⲙⲁⲩ ⲁϥⲙⲟⲩ ⲡⲉⲧⲉⲙ̄ ⲙⲁϫⲉ

10 ⲙ̄ⲙⲟϥ` ⲙⲁⲣⲉϥ`ⲥⲱⲧⲙ̄ (64) ⲡⲉϫⲉ ⲓ̄ⲥ̄ ϫⲉ ⲟⲩⲣⲱ

ⲙⲉ ⲛⲉⲩⲛ̄ⲧⲁϥ ϩⲛ̄ϣⲙ̄ⲙⲟ ⲁⲩⲱ ⲛ̄ⲧⲁⲣⲉϥⲥⲟⲃ

30 ⲡⲉϫⲉ ⲥⲁⲗⲱⲙⲏ ϫⲉ (or the like) is omitted before ⲁⲛⲟⲕ

31 ⲡⲉϫⲉ ⲓ̄ⲥ̄ ⲛⲁⲥ ϫⲉ (or the like) is omitted after ⲙⲁⲑⲏⲧⲏⲥ

32 ϣⲏϥ *sic*; *l.* ϣⲏϣ ?

35 *cf.* BG 32, 18/19

5 ⲱϭ: after ⲱ there is ϩ cancelled by a horizontal stroke

24 on a bed: the one will die, the one
will live.　Salome said: Who art thou,

26 man, and (ὡς) whose (son)? Thou didst take thy place upon
my bench and eat from my

28 table (τράπεζα). Jesus said to her: I am He
who is from the Same,

30 to Me was given from the things of My Father. ‹Salome said›: I
am Thy disciple (μαθητής). ‹Jesus said to her›: Therefore I say,

32 if (ὅταν) he is the Same, he will be filled
with light, but (δέ) if (ὅταν) he is

34 divided, he will be filled with darkness. (62) Jesus said: I
tell My mysteries (μυστήριον) to those [who are worthy

92 of my] mysteries (μυστήριον).　What thy right (hand) will do,

2 let not thy left (hand) know what it does. (63) Jesus said:
There was a rich (πλούσιος) man who had

4 much money (χρῆμα). He said: I will use (χρῆσθαι)
my money (χρῆμα) that I may sow and reap

6 and plant and fill my storehouses with fruit (καρπός),
so that (ἵνα) I lack nothing. This was

8 what he thought in his heart. And
that night he died. Whoever has ears

10 let him hear. (64) Jesus said: A man
had guest-friends, and when he had prepared

26 Lit: as from whom (ὡς ἐκ τίνος;). Ms.: as from somebody (ὡς ἐκ τινός).

12 ⲧⲉ ⲙ̄ⲡⲇⲓⲡⲛⲟⲛ ⲁϥϫⲟⲟⲩ ⲙ̄ⲡⲉϥϩⲙ̄ϩⲁⲗ̄ ϣⲓ
ⲛⲁ ⲉϥⲛⲁⲧⲱϩⲙ̄ ⲛ̄ⲛ̄ϣⲙ̄ⲙⲟⲉⲓ ⲁϥⲃⲱⲕ` ⲙ̄

14 ⲡϣⲟⲣⲡ` ⲡⲉϫⲁϥ ⲛⲁϥ ϫⲉ ⲡⲁϫⲟⲉⲓⲥ ⲧⲱ̄ϩ̄
ⲙ̄ⲙⲟⲕ· ⲡⲉϫⲁϥ ϫⲉ ⲟⲩⲛ̄ⲧⲁⲉⲓ ϩⲛ̄ϩⲣⲟⲙⲧ`

16 ⲁⲣⲉⲛⲉⲙⲡⲟⲣⲟⲥ ⲥⲉⲛⲛⲏⲧ ϣⲁⲣⲟⲉⲓ ⲉⲣⲟⲩⲧⲉ
ϯⲛⲁⲃⲱⲕ` ⲛ̄ⲧⲁⲟⲩⲉϩⲥⲁϩⲛⲉ ⲛⲁⲩ ϯⲣ̄ⲡⲁⲣⲁⲓ

18 ⲧⲉⲓ ⲙ̄ⲡⲇⲓⲡⲛⲟⲛ ⲁϥⲃⲱⲕ` ϣⲁ ⲕⲉⲟⲩⲁ ⲡⲉ
ϫⲁϥ ⲛⲁϥ ϫⲉ ⲁⲡⲁϫⲟⲉⲓⲥ ⲧⲱϩ̄ ⲙ̄ⲙⲟⲕ`

20 ⲡⲉϫⲁϥ ⲛⲁϥ ϫⲉ ⲁⲉⲓⲧⲟⲟⲩ ⲟⲩⲛⲉⲓ ⲁⲩⲱ ⲥⲉ
ⲣⲁⲓⲧⲉⲓ ⲙ̄ⲙⲟⲉⲓ ⲛ̄ⲟⲩⲏⲙⲉⲣⲁ ϯⲛⲁⲥⲣ̄ϥⲉ ⲁ

22 ⲁϥⲉⲓ ϣⲁ ⲕⲉⲟⲩⲁ ⲡⲉϫⲁϥ ⲛⲁϥ ϫⲉ ⲡⲁϫⲟ
ⲉⲓⲥ ⲧⲱϩ̄ ⲙ̄ⲙⲟⲕ` ⲡⲉϫⲁϥ ⲛⲁϥ ϫⲉ ⲡⲁϣⲃⲏⲣ

24 ⲛⲁⲣ̄ ϣⲉⲗⲉⲉⲧ ⲁⲩⲱ ⲁⲛⲟⲕ· ⲉⲧⲛⲁⲣ ⲇⲓⲡⲛⲟⲛ
ϯⲛⲁϣ ⲓ ⲁⲛ ϯⲣ̄ⲡⲁⲣⲁⲓⲧⲉⲓ ⲙ̄ⲡⲇⲓⲡⲛⲟⲛ· ⲁϥ`

26 ⲃⲱⲕ` ϣⲁ ⲕⲉⲟⲩⲁ ⲡⲉϫⲁϥ ⲛⲁϥ ϫⲉ ⲡⲁϫⲟⲉⲓⲥ
ⲧⲱϩ̄ ⲙ̄ⲙⲟⲕ` ⲡⲉϫⲁϥ ⲛⲁϥ` ϫⲉ ⲁⲉⲓⲧⲟⲟⲩ ⲛ̄

28 ⲟⲩⲕⲱⲙⲏ ⲉⲉⲓⲃⲏⲕ` ⲁϫⲓ ⲛ̄ϣⲱⲙ ϯⲛⲁϣ ⲓ
ⲁⲛ ϯⲣ̄ⲡⲁⲣⲁⲓⲧⲉⲓ ⲁϥⲉⲓ ⲛ̄ϭⲓ ⲡϩⲙ̄ϩⲁⲗ̄ ⲁϥϫⲟ

30 ⲟⲥ ⲁⲡⲉϥϫⲟⲉⲓⲥ ϫⲉ ⲛⲉⲛⲧⲁⲕ`ⲧⲁϩⲙⲟⲩ ⲁ
ⲡⲇⲓⲡⲛⲟⲛ ⲁⲩⲡⲁⲣⲁⲓⲧⲉⲓ ⲡⲉϫⲉ ⲡϫⲟⲉⲓⲥ ⲙ̄

32 ⲡⲉϥϩⲙ̄ϩⲁⲗ̄ ϫⲉ ⲃⲱⲕ` ⲉⲡⲥⲁ ⲛⲃⲟⲗ ⲁⲛϩⲓⲟ
ⲟⲩⲉ ⲛⲉⲧⲕⲛⲁϩⲉ ⲉⲣⲟⲟⲩ ⲉⲛⲓⲟⲩ ϫⲉⲕⲁⲁⲥ

34 ⲉⲩⲛⲁⲣ̄ⲇⲓⲡⲛⲉⲓ ⲛ̄ⲣⲉϥⲧⲟⲟⲩ ⲙⲛ̄ ⲛⲉϣⲟ
[ⲧⲉ ⲉⲩⲛⲁⲃⲱ]ⲕ ⲁⲛ` ⲉϩⲟⲩⲛ` ⲉⲛⲧⲟⲡⲟⲥ ⲙ̄ⲡⲁⲓⲱⲧ`

36

12 the dinner (δεῖπνον), he sent his servant to (ἵνα)
invite the guest-friends. He went to

14 the first, he said to him: "My master invites
thee". He said: "I have some claims

16 against some merchants (ἔμπορος); they will come to me in the evening;
I will go and give them my orders. I pray to be excused (παραιτεῖσθαι)

18 from the dinner (δεῖπνον)". He went to another,
he said to him: "My master has invited thee".

20 He said to him: "I have bought a house and they
request (αἰτεῖν) me for a day (ἡμέρα). I will have no time".

22 He came to another, he said to him: "My master
invites thee". He said to him: "My friend

24 is to be married and I am to arrange a dinner (δεῖπνον);
I shall not be able to come. I pray to be excused (παραιτεῖσθαι) from the

26 He went to another, he said to him: "My master [dinner" (δεῖπνον).
invites thee". He said to him: "I have bought

28 a farm (κώμη), I go to collect the rent. I shall not be able to come.
I pray to be excused" (παραιτεῖσθαι). The servant came, he said

30 to his master: "Those whom thou hast invited to
the dinner (δεῖπνον) have excused (παραιτεῖσθαι) themselves". The

32 his servant: "Go out to the roads,   [master said to
bring those whom thou shalt find, so that

34 they may dine (δειπνεῖν). Tradesmen and merchants
[shall] not [enter] the places (τόπος) of my Father".

21 "me for a day", or "a day from me".

93   (65) пехас̄ ж̄е оꙋр̄ω̄ме ̄н̄х̄рн[ст]о̄с нетн̄[тас̄]

2   ноꙋм̄а нел̄ооле ас̄таас̄ н̄[ꙅ]ноꙋоеіе
    щіна етнар̄ ꙅω̄в̄ ерос̄ н̄с̄ж̄і ̄м̄пес̄кар̄

4   пос н̄тоотоꙋ ас̄ж̄ооꙋ ̄м̄пес̄ꙅм̄ꙅал̄ ж̄е
    каас еноꙋоеіе на† нас̄ ̄м̄пкарпос ̄м̄

6   пл̄а нел̄ооле аꙋем̄арте ̄м̄пес̄ꙅм̄ꙅал̄
    аꙋꙅіоꙋе ерос̄ некекоꙋеі пе н̄сем̄ооꙋтс̄

8   апꙅм̄ꙅал̄ вω̄к̄ ас̄ж̄оос епес̄ж̄оеіс пе
    ж̄е пес̄ж̄оеіс ж̄е м̄ещак̄ ̄м̄пес̄сотω̄

10   ноꙋ ас̄ж̄ооꙋ н̄кеꙅм̄ꙅал̄ аноꙋоеіе ꙅі
    оꙋе епкеꙅта тоте апж̄оеіс ж̄ооꙋ ̄м̄

12   пес̄щнре пехас̄ ж̄е м̄ещак̄ сенащіпе
    ꙅнтс̄ ̄м̄пащнре ан̄оꙋоеіе етм̄м̄аꙋ епеі

14   сесооꙋн ж̄е н̄тос̄ пе пекл̄нроном̄ос
    ̄м̄пл̄а нел̄ооле аꙋꙅопс̄ аꙋм̄ооꙋтс̄

16   петет̄м̄ м̄ааж̄е ̄м̄мос̄ м̄арес̄сωт̄м̄ (66) пе
    ж̄е іс̄ ж̄е м̄атсевоеі епωне паеі н̄таꙋ

18   стос̄ евол̄ н̄с̄і нет̄кωт̄ н̄тос̄ пе пω̄
    не н̄кωꙅ (67) пехе іс̄ ж̄е петсооꙋн ̄м̄птнрс̄

20   ес̄р̄ ꙅрω̄ꙅ оꙋаас̄ р̄ ꙅрω̄ꙅ ̄м̄пл̄а тнрс̄
    (68) пеж̄е іс̄ ж̄е н̄тω̄тн̄ ꙅм̄макаріос ꙅотa̅

22   еꙋщанместе тнꙋтн̄ н̄серж̄іω̄ке ̄м̄
    мω̄тн̄ аꙋω̄ сенаꙅе ан етопос ꙅm̄ пл̄а

24   ентаꙋж̄іω̄ке ̄м̄мω̄тн̄ ꙅраі н̄ꙅнтс̄ (69) пе

9/10 ̄м̄пес̄соꙋω̄ноꙋ probably for ̄м̄поꙋсоꙋω̄нс̄

93   (65) He said: A good (χρηστός) man had

2 a vineyard. He gave it to husbandmen

so that (ἵνα) they would work it and that he would receive its fruit

4 from them. He sent his servant so that   [(καρπός)

the husbandmen would give him the fruit (καρπός) of

6 the vineyard. They seized his servant,

they beat him; a little longer and they would have killed him.

8 The servant came, he told it to his master.

His master said: "Perhaps he did not know them".

10 He sent another servant; the husbandmen beat

him as well. Then (τότε) the owner sent

12 his son. He said: "Perhaps they will respect

my son". Since (ἐπεί) those husbandmen

14 knew that he was the heir (κληρονόμος)

of the vineyard, they seized him, they killed him.

16 Whoever has ears let him hear.

(66) Jesus said: Show me the stone which

18 the builders have rejected; it is the corner-stone.

(67) Jesus said: Whoever knows the All

20 but fails (to know) himself lacks everything.

(68) Jesus said: Blessed (μακάριος) are you when (ὅταν)

22 you are hated and persecuted (διώκειν);

and no place (τόπος) will be found there

24 where you have been persecuted (διώκειν).

9 read: "perhaps they did not recognize him".
23-24 read: "you will find a place, where you will not be persecuted".

ϫⲉ ⲓ̅ⲥ̅ ϩⲙ̅ⲙⲁⲕⲁⲣⲓⲟⲥ ⲛⲉ ⲛⲁⲉⲓ ⲛ̅ⲧⲁⲩⲇⲓⲱⲕⲉ

26 ⲙ̅ⲙⲟⲟⲩ ϩⲣⲁⲓ̈ ϩⲙ̅ ⲡⲟⲩϩⲏⲧ' ⲛⲉⲧⲙ̅ⲙⲁⲩ'

ⲛⲉⲛⲧⲁϩⲥⲟⲩⲱⲛ ⲡⲉⲓⲱⲧ' ϩⲛ̅ ⲟⲩⲙⲉ ϩⲛ̅

28 ⲙⲁⲕⲁⲣⲓⲟⲥ ⲛⲉⲧϩⲕⲁⲉⲓⲧ' ϣⲓⲛⲁ ⲉⲧⲛⲁ

ⲧⲥⲓⲟ ⲛ̅ⲑⲣⲏ ⲙ̅ⲡⲉⲧⲟⲩⲱϣ (70) ⲡⲉϫⲉ ⲓ̅ⲥ̅ ϩⲟ

30 ⲧⲁⲛ ⲉⲧⲉⲧⲛ̅ϣⲁϫⲡⲉ ⲡⲏ ϩⲛ̅ ⲧⲏⲩⲧⲛ̅ ⲡⲁⲓ̈

ⲉⲧⲉⲩⲛ̅ⲧⲏⲧⲛ̅ϥ ϥⲛⲁⲧⲟⲩϫⲉ ⲧⲏⲩⲧⲛ̅ ⲉϣⲱ

32 ⲡⲉ ⲙ̅ⲛⲧⲏⲧⲛ̅ ⲡⲏ ϩⲛ̅ [ⲧⲏⲩ]ⲧⲛ̅ ⲡⲁⲉⲓ ⲉⲧⲉ

ⲙ̅ⲛⲧⲏⲧⲛ̅ϥ ϩⲛ̅ ⲧⲏⲛⲉ ϥ[ⲛⲁⲙ]ⲟⲩⲧ' ⲧⲏⲛⲉ

34 (71) ⲡⲉϫⲉ ⲓ̅ⲥ̅ ϫⲉ ϯⲛⲁϣⲟⲣ[ϣⲣ ⲙ̅ⲡⲉⲉⲓ]ⲏⲉⲓ

ⲁⲩⲱ ⲙⲛ̅ ⲗⲁⲁⲩ ⲛⲁϣ ⲕⲟⲧϥ̅ [ⲁⲛ ⲛ̅ⲕⲉⲥⲟ]ⲡ

94 (72) [ⲡⲉϫ]ⲉ ⲟ[ⲩⲣⲱⲙⲉ] ⲛⲁϥ ϫⲉ ϫⲟⲟⲥ ⲛ̅ⲛⲁⲥⲛⲏⲩ

2 ϣⲓⲛⲁ ⲉⲧⲛ[ⲁ]ⲡⲱϣⲉ ⲛ̅ⲛϩⲛⲁⲁⲩ ⲙ̅ⲡⲁⲉⲓⲱⲧ'

ⲛⲙ̅ⲙⲁⲉⲓ ⲡⲉϫⲁϥ ⲛⲁϥ ϫⲉ ⲱ ⲡⲣⲱⲙⲉ ⲛⲓⲙ

4 ⲡⲉ ⲛ̅ⲧⲁϩⲁⲁⲧ' ⲛ̅ⲣⲉϥⲡⲱϣⲉ ⲁϥⲕⲟⲧϥ̅ ⲁ'

ⲛⲉϥⲙⲁⲑⲏⲧⲏⲥ ⲡⲉϫⲁϥ ⲛⲁⲩ ϫⲉ ⲙⲏ ⲉⲉⲓ

6 ϣⲟⲟⲡ' ⲛ̅ⲣⲉϥ'ⲡⲱϣⲉ (73) ⲡⲉϫⲉ ⲓ̅ⲥ̅ ϫⲉ ⲡⲱⲥ

ⲙⲉⲛ ⲛⲁϣⲱϥ' ⲛ̅ⲉⲣⲅⲁⲧⲏⲥ ⲇⲉ ⲥⲟⲃⲕ' ⲥⲟⲡⲥ̅

8 ⲇⲉ ⲙ̅ⲡϫⲟⲉⲓⲥ ϣⲓⲛⲁ ⲉϥⲛⲁⲛⲉϫ' ⲉⲣⲅⲁⲧⲏⲥ

ⲉⲃⲟⲗ' ⲉⲡⲱϩⲥ̅ (74) ⲡⲉϫⲁϥ ϫⲉ ⲡϫⲟⲉⲓⲥ ⲟⲩⲛ̅

10 ϩⲁϩ ⲙ̅ⲡⲕⲱⲧⲉ ⲛ̅ⲧϫⲱⲧⲉ ⲙⲛ̅ ⲗⲁⲁⲩ ⲇⲉ ϩⲛ̅

ⲧϣⲱⲛⲉ· (75) ⲡⲉϫⲉ ⲓ̅ⲥ̅ ⲟⲩⲛ̅ ϩⲁϩ ⲁϩⲉⲣⲁⲧⲟⲩ

12 ϩⲓⲣⲙ̅ ⲡⲣⲟ ⲁⲗⲗⲁ ⲙ̅ⲙⲟⲛⲁⲭⲟⲥ ⲛⲉⲧⲛⲁⲃⲱⲕ'

ⲉϩⲟⲩⲛ ⲉⲡⲙⲁ ⲛ̅ϣⲉⲗⲉⲉⲧ' (76) ⲡⲉϫⲉ ⲓ̅ⲥ̅ ϫⲉ

29 ⲛ̅ⲑⲣⲏ ⲙ̅ⲡⲉⲧⲟⲩⲱϣ should probably be ⲛ̅ϩⲏⲧⲟⲩ ⲙ̅ⲡⲉⲧⲟⲩⲟⲩⲁ-
ϣϥ

10 ⲧϫⲱⲧⲉ *sic*; *l.* ⲧϣⲱⲧⲉ

11 ⲧϣⲱⲛⲉ *sic*; *l.* ⲧϣⲱⲧⲉ

(69a) Jesus said: Blessed (μακάριος) are those who have been persecuted

26 in their heart; these are they   [(διώκειν)

who have known the Father in truth.

28 (69b) Blessed (μακάριος) are the hungry, for (ἵνα)

the belly of him who desires will be filled. (70) Jesus said:

30 If (ὅταν) you bring forth that within yourselves,

that which you have will save you.

32 If you do not have that within yourselves,

that which you do not have within you will kill you.

34 (71) Jesus said: I shall de[stroy this] house

and no one will be able to build it [again].

94   (72) [A man said] to Him: Tell my brethren

2 to (ἵνα) divide my father's possessions

with me. He said to him: O (ὦ) man, who

4 made Me (a) divider? He turned to

His disciples (μαθητής), he said to them: I am not a divider,

6 am I (μή)? (73) Jesus said: The harvest

is indeed (μέν) great, but (δέ) the labourers (ἐργάτης) are few;

8 but (δέ) beg the Lord to (ἵνα) send labourers (ἐργάτης)

into the harvest. (74) He said: Lord, there are

10 many around the cistern, but (δέ) nobody in

the cistern. (75) Jesus said: Many are standing

12 at the door, but (ἀλλά) the solitary (μοναχός) are the ones who will

the bridal chamber. (76) Jesus said: [enter

29 possibly: "they will fill their belly with what they desire".

41

14 ⲧⲙⲛⲧⲉⲣⲟ ⲙ̄ⲡⲉⲓⲱⲧ ⲉⲥⲧⲛ̄ⲧⲱⲛ ⲁⲩⲣⲱⲙⲉ
ⲛⲉϣ̄ϣⲱⲧ ⲉⲩⲛ̄ⲧⲁϥ ⲙ̄ⲙⲁⲩ ⲛ̄ⲟⲩⲫⲟⲣⲧⲓ

16 ⲟⲛ ⲉⲁϥϩⲉ ⲁⲩⲙⲁⲣⲅⲁⲣⲓⲧⲏⲥ ⲡⲉϣⲱⲧ
ⲉⲧⲙ̄ⲙⲁⲩ ⲟⲩⲥⲁⲃⲉ ⲡⲉ ⲁϥϯ ⲡⲉϥⲫⲟⲣⲧⲓⲟⲛ

18 ⲉⲃⲟⲗ ⲁϥⲧⲟⲟⲩ ⲛⲁϥ ⲙ̄ⲡⲓⲙⲁⲣⲅⲁⲣⲓⲧⲏⲥ
ⲟⲩⲱⲧ ⲛ̄ⲧⲱⲧⲛ̄ ϩⲱⲧ ⲧⲏⲩⲧⲛ̄ ϣⲓⲛⲉ ⲛ̄

20 ⲥⲁ ⲡⲉϥⲉϩⲟ ⲉⲙⲁϥϣⲱϫⲛ ⲉϥⲙⲏⲛ ⲉⲃⲟⲗ
ⲡⲙⲁ ⲉⲙⲁⲣⲉϫⲟⲟⲗⲉⲥ ⲧϩⲛⲟ ⲉϩⲟⲩⲛ ⲉⲙⲁⲩ

22 ⲉⲟⲩⲱⲙ ⲟⲩⲇⲉ ⲙⲁⲣⲉϥϥⲛ̄ⲧ ⲧⲁⲕⲟ (77) ⲡⲉϫⲉ
ⲓ̄ⲥ̄ ϫⲉ ⲁⲛⲟⲕ ⲡⲉ ⲡⲟⲩⲟⲉⲓⲛ ⲡⲁⲉⲓ ⲉⲧϩⲓ

24 ϫⲱⲟⲩ ⲧⲏⲣⲟⲩ ⲁⲛⲟⲕ ⲡⲉ ⲡⲧⲏⲣϥ ⲛ̄ⲧⲁ
ⲡⲧⲏⲣϥ ⲉⲓ ⲉⲃⲟⲗ ⲛ̄ϩⲏⲧ ⲁⲩⲱ ⲛ̄ⲧⲁⲡⲧⲏⲣϥ

26 ⲡⲱϩ ϣⲁⲣⲟⲉⲓ ⲡⲱϩ ⲛ̄ⲛⲟⲩϣⲉ ⲁⲛⲟⲕ
ϯⲙ̄ⲙⲁⲩ ϥⲓ ⲙ̄ⲡⲱⲛⲉ ⲉϩⲣⲁⲓ̈ ⲁⲩⲱ ⲧⲉⲧⲛⲁ

28 ϩⲉ ⲉⲣⲟⲉⲓ ⲙ̄ⲙⲁⲩ (78) ⲡⲉϫⲉ ⲓ̄ⲥ̄ ϫⲉ ⲉⲧⲃⲉ ⲟⲩ
ⲁⲧⲉⲧⲛⲉⲓ ⲉⲃⲟⲗ ⲉⲧⲥⲱϣⲉ ⲉⲛⲁⲩ ⲉⲩⲕⲁϣ

30 ⲉϥⲕⲓⲙ ⲉ[ⲃⲟⲗ] ϩⲓⲧⲙ̄ ⲡⲧⲏⲩ ⲁⲩⲱ ⲉⲛⲁⲩ
ⲉⲩⲣ[ⲱⲙⲉ ⲉϩ]ⲛ̄ϣⲧⲏⲛ ⲉⲩϭⲏⲛ ϩⲓⲱⲱϥ·

32 [ⲉⲓⲥ ⲛⲉⲧⲛ̄]ⲣ̄ⲣⲱⲟⲩ ⲙⲛ̄ ⲛⲉⲧⲙ̄ⲙⲉⲅⲓ

95 ⲥⲧⲁⲛⲟⲥ ⲛⲁⲉⲓ ⲉⲛ[ϣⲧⲏ]ⲛ [ⲉⲧ]

2 ϭⲏⲛ ϩⲓⲱⲟⲩ ⲁⲩⲱ ⲥⲉ[ⲛⲁ]ϣ ⲥⲟⲩⲛ
ⲧⲙⲉ ⲁⲛ (79) ⲡⲉϫⲉ ⲟⲩⲥϩⲓⲙ[ⲉ] ⲛⲁϥ ϩⲙ̄

4 ⲡⲙⲏϣⲉ ϫⲉ ⲛⲉⲉⲓⲁⲧ[ⲥ ⲛ̄]ⲑ̄ϩ ⲛ̄
ⲧⲁϥϥⲓ ϩⲁⲣⲟⲕ ⲁⲩⲱ ⲛ̄ⲕⲓ[ⲃ]ⲉ ⲉⲛⲧⲁϩ

20 ⲡⲉϥⲉϩⲟ ('his treasure'): at first ⲡⲉϥϩⲟ ('his face') to which the second
ⲉ was added. Correct is ⲡⲉϩⲟ

22 ⲙⲁⲣⲉϥϥⲛ̄ⲧ sic; l. ⲙⲁⲣⲉϥϭⲛ̄ⲧ

42

14 The Kingdom of the Father is like a man,
a merchant, who possessed merchandise (φορτίον)

16 (and) found a pearl (μαργαρίτης). That merchant
was prudent. He sold the merchandise (φορτίον),

18 he bought the one pearl (μαργαρίτης) for himself.
Do you also seek for

20 the treasure which fails not, which endures,
there where no moth comes near

22 to devour and (where) no (οὐδέ) worm destroys.
(77) Jesus said: I am the Light that is above

24 them all, I am the All,
the All came forth from Me and the All

26 attained to Me. Cleave a (piece of) wood, I
am there; lift up the stone and you will

28 find Me there. (78) Jesus said: Why
did you come out into the desert? To see a reed

30 shaken by the wind? And to see
a man clothed in soft garments?

32 [See, your] kings and your great ones (μεγιστᾶνος)

95 are those who are clothed in soft [garments]

2 and they [shall] not be able to know the truth.
(79) A woman from the multitude said to Him:

4 Blessed is the womb which
bore Thee and the breasts which

6 ⲥⲁϩⲛⲟⲧⲩⲕ ⲡⲉϫⲁϥ ⲛⲁ[ⲥ] ϫⲉ ⲛⲉ
 ⲉⲓⲁⲧⲟⲩ ⲛ̄ⲛⲉⲛⲧⲁⲣⲥⲱⲧⲙ̄ ⲁ⁚

8 ⲡⲗⲟⲅⲟⲥ ⲙ̄ⲡⲉⲓⲱⲧ ⲁⲩⲁⲣⲉϩ ⲉⲣⲟϥ
 ϩⲛ ⲟⲩⲙⲉ ⲟⲩⲛ ϩⲛϩⲟⲟⲩ ⲅⲁⲣ ⲛⲁϣⲱⲡⲉ

10 ⲛ̄ⲧⲉⲧⲛ̄ϫⲟⲟⲥ ϫⲉ ⲛⲉⲉⲓⲁⲧⲥ ⲛ̄ⲑⲟⲛ ⲧⲁ
 ⲉⲓ ⲉⲧⲉ ⲙ̄ⲡⲥⲱ ⲁⲩⲱ ⲛ̄ⲕⲓⲃⲉ ⲛⲁⲉⲓ ⲉⲙⲡⲟⲩ

12 † ⲉⲣⲱⲧⲉ (80) ⲡⲉϫⲉ ⲓⲥ ϫⲉ ⲡⲉⲛⲧⲁⲣⲥⲟⲩⲱⲛ
 ⲡⲕⲟⲥⲙⲟⲥ ⲁϥϩⲉ ⲉⲡⲥⲱⲙⲁ ⲡⲉⲛⲧⲁϩϩⲉ

14 ⲇⲉ ⲉⲡⲥⲱⲙⲁ ⲡⲕⲟⲥⲙⲟⲥ ⲙ̄ⲡϣⲁ ⲙ̄ⲙⲟϥ⸱
 ⲁⲛ⸱ (81) ⲡⲉϫⲉ ⲓⲥ ϫⲉ ⲡⲉⲛⲧⲁϩⲣ ⲣⲙⲙⲁⲟ ⲙⲁ

16 ⲣⲉϥⲣ ⲣⲣⲟ ⲁⲩⲱ ⲡⲉⲧⲩⲛ̄ⲧⲁϥ ⲛ̄ⲟⲩⲇⲩⲛⲁ
 ⲙⲓⲥ ⲙⲁⲣⲉϥⲁⲣⲛⲁ (82) ⲡⲉϫⲉ ⲓⲥ ϫⲉ ⲡⲉⲧϩⲏⲛ

18 ⲉⲣⲟⲉⲓ ⲉϥϩⲏⲛ ⲉⲧⲥⲁⲧⲉ ⲁⲩⲱ ⲡⲉⲧⲟⲩⲏⲩ⸱
 ⲙ̄ⲙⲟⲉⲓ ϥⲟⲩⲏⲩ ⲛ̄ⲧⲙⲛⲧⲉⲣⲟ (83) ⲡⲉϫⲉ ⲓⲥ

20 ϫⲉ ⲛ̄ϩⲓⲕⲱⲛ ⲥⲉⲟⲩⲟⲛϩ ⲉⲃⲟⲗ ⲙ̄ⲡⲣⲱ
 ⲙⲉ ⲁⲩⲱ ⲡⲟⲩⲟⲉⲓⲛ ⲉⲧⲛ̄ϩⲏⲧⲟⲩ ϥϩⲏⲡ⸱

22 ϩⲛ ⲑⲓⲕⲱⲛ ⲙ̄ⲡⲟⲩⲟⲉⲓⲛ ⲙ̄ⲡⲉⲓⲱⲧ⸱ ϥⲛⲁ
 ϭⲱⲗⲡ⸱ ⲉⲃⲟⲗ ⲁⲩⲱ ⲧⲉϥϩⲓⲕⲱⲛ ϩⲏⲡ⸱

24 ⲉⲃⲟⲗ ϩⲓⲧⲛ̄ ⲡⲉϥ⸱ⲟⲩⲟⲉⲓⲛ (84) ⲡⲉϫⲉ ⲓⲥ ⲛ̄ϩⲟ
 ⲟⲩ ⲉⲧⲉⲧⲛ̄ⲛⲁⲩ ⲉⲡⲉⲧⲛ̄ⲉⲓⲛⲉ ϣⲁⲣⲉⲧⲛ̄

26 ⲣⲁϣⲉ ϩⲟⲧⲁⲛ ⲇⲉ ⲉⲧⲉⲧⲛ̄ϣⲁⲛⲛⲁⲩ⸱
 ⲁⲛⲉⲧⲛ̄ϩⲓⲕⲱⲛ⸱ ⲛ̄ⲧⲁϩϣⲱⲡⲉ ϩⲓ ⲧⲉⲧⲛ̄ⲉ

28 ϩⲛ ⲟⲩⲧⲉ ⲙⲁⲩⲙⲟⲩ ⲟⲩⲧⲉ ⲙⲁⲩⲟⲩⲱⲛϩ
 ⲉⲃⲟⲗ ⲧⲉⲧⲛⲁϥⲓ ϩⲁ ⲟⲩⲏⲣ⸱ (85) ⲡⲉϫⲉ ⲓⲥ ϫⲉ

30 ⲛ̄ⲧⲁⲁⲇⲁⲙ ϣⲱⲡⲉ ⲉⲃⲟⲗ ϩⲛ̄ ⲟⲩⲛⲟϭ

6 ⲥⲁϩⲛⲟⲧⲩⲕ *sic; l.* ⲥⲁⲛⲟⲩⲕ

44

6 nourished Thee. He said to [her]:

Blessed are those who have heard

8 the word (λόγος) of the Father (and) have kept it

in truth. For (γάρ) there will be days

10 when you will say: Blessed is the womb

which has not conceived and the breasts which have not suckled.

12 (80) Jesus said: Whoever has known

the world (κόσμος) has found the body (σῶμα), and (δέ) whoever has

14 the body (σῶμα), of him the world (κόσμος) is not worthy.   [found

(81) Jesus said: Let him who has become rich

16 become king, and let him who has power (δύναμις)

renounce (ἀρνεῖσθαι) (it). (82) Jesus said: Whoever is near

18 to me is near to the fire, and whoever is far

from me is far from the Kingdom. (83) Jesus said:

20 The images (εἰκών) are manifest to man

and the Light which is within them is hidden

22 in the Image (εἰκών) of the Light of the Father.

He will manifest himself and His Image (εἰκών) is concealed

24 by His Light. (84) Jesus said:

When you see your likeness, you

26 rejoice. But (δέ) when (ὅταν) you see

your images (εἰκών) which came into existence before you,

28 (which) neither (οὔτε) die nor (οὔτε) are manifested,

how much will you bear! (85) Jesus said:

30 Adam came into existence from a great

---

29 Exclamation or question.

ⲛⲁⲩⲛⲁⲙⲓⲥ ⲙⲛ ⲟⲩⲛⲟϭ ⲙⲙⲛⲧⲣⲙⲙⲁ

32 ⲟ ⲁⲩⲱ ⲙⲡⲉϥϣⲱⲡⲉ ⲉ[ϥⲙⲡ]ϣⲁ ⲙⲙⲱ

ⲧⲛ ⲛⲉⲧⲁϫⲓⲟⲥ ⲅⲁⲣ ⲡⲉ [ⲛⲉϥⲛⲁϫⲓ ϯⲡ[ⲉ]

34 ⲁⲛ ⲙⲡⲙⲟⲩ (86) ⲡⲉϫⲉ ⲓⲥ ϫⲉ [ⲛⲃⲁϣⲟⲣ ⲟⲩ

ⲛⲧⲁ]ⲩ ⲛ[ⲉⲩⲃⲏⲃ] ⲁⲩⲱ ⲛϩⲁⲗⲁⲧⲉ ⲟⲩⲛⲧⲁⲩ

2 ⲙⲙⲁⲩ ⲙ[ⲡⲉ]ⲩⲙⲁϩ ⲡϣⲏⲣⲉ ⲇⲉ ⲙⲡⲣⲱⲙⲉ

ⲙⲛⲧⲁϥ ⲛⲛ[ⲟⲩ]ⲙⲁ ⲉⲣⲓⲕⲉ ⲛⲧⲉϥ·ⲁⲡⲉ ⲛϥ·

4 ⲙⲧⲟⲛ ⲙ[ⲙⲟ]ϥ (87) ⲡⲉϫⲁϥ ⲛϭⲓ ⲓⲥ ϫⲉ ⲟⲩⲧⲁⲗⲁⲓ

ⲡⲱⲣⲟⲛ ⲡ[ⲉ] ⲡⲥⲱⲙⲁ ⲉⲧⲁϣⲉ ⲛⲟⲩⲥⲱⲙⲁ

6 ⲁⲩⲱ ⲟⲩⲧ[ⲁ]ⲗⲁⲓⲡⲱⲣⲟⲥ ⲧⲉ ⲧ·ⲯⲩⲭⲏ ⲉⲧⲁϣⲉ

ⲛⲛⲁⲉⲓ ⲙⲡⲥⲛⲁⲩ (88) ⲡⲉϫⲉ ⲓⲥ ϫⲉ ⲛⲁⲅⲅⲉⲗⲟⲥ

8 ⲛⲏⲩ ϣⲁⲣⲱⲧⲛ ⲙⲛ ⲛⲡⲣⲟⲫⲏⲧⲏⲥ ⲁⲩⲱ ⲥⲉ

ⲛⲁϯ ⲛⲏⲧⲛ ⲛⲛⲉⲧⲉⲩⲛⲧⲏⲧⲛⲥⲉ ⲁⲩⲱ·

10 ⲛⲧⲱⲧⲛ ϩⲱⲧ ⲧⲏⲩⲧⲛ ⲛⲉⲧⲛⲧⲟⲧ· ⲧⲏⲛⲉ

ⲧⲁⲁⲩ ⲛⲁⲩ ⲛⲧⲉⲧⲛϫⲟⲟⲥ ⲛⲏⲧⲛ ϫⲉ ⲁϣ ⲛ

12 ϩⲟⲟⲩ ⲡⲉⲧⲟⲩⲛⲛⲏⲩ ⲛⲥⲉϫⲓ ⲡⲉⲧⲉ ⲡⲱⲟⲩ

(89) ⲡⲉϫⲉ ⲓⲥ ϫⲉ ⲉⲧⲃⲉ ⲟⲩ ⲧⲉⲧⲛⲉⲓⲱⲉ ⲙⲡⲥⲁ ⲛ

14 ⲃⲟⲗ· ⲙⲡⲡⲟⲧⲏⲣⲓⲟⲛ ⲧⲉⲧⲛⲣⲛⲟⲉⲓ ⲁⲛ ϫⲉ

ⲡⲉⲛⲧⲁϩⲧⲁⲙⲓⲟ ⲙⲡⲥⲁ ⲛϩⲟⲩⲛ ⲛⲧⲟϥ ⲟⲛ

16 ⲡⲉⲛⲧⲁϥⲧⲁⲙⲓⲟ ⲙⲡⲥⲁ ⲛⲃⲟⲗ· (90) ⲡⲉϫⲉ ⲓⲏⲥ

ϫⲉ ⲁⲙⲛⲉⲓⲧⲛ ϣⲁⲣⲟⲉⲓ· ϫⲉ ⲟⲩⲭⲣⲏⲥⲧⲟⲥ

18 ⲡⲉ ⲡⲁⲛⲁϩⲃ· ⲁⲩⲱ ⲧⲁⲙⲛⲧϫⲟⲉⲓⲥ ⲟⲩⲣⲙ

ⲣⲁϣ ⲧⲉ ⲁⲩⲱ ⲧⲉⲧⲛⲁϩⲉ ⲁⲩⲁⲛⲁⲡⲁⲥⲓⲥ ⲛⲏ

20 ⲧⲛ (91) ⲡⲉϫⲁⲩ ⲛⲁϥ· ϫⲉ ϫⲟⲟⲥ ⲉⲣⲟⲛ ϫⲉ

ⲛⲧⲕ ⲛⲓⲙ ϣⲓⲛⲁ ⲉⲛⲁⲣⲡⲓⲥⲧⲉⲩⲉ ⲉⲣⲟⲕ· ⲡⲉ

power (δύναμις) and a great wealth,

32 and (yet) he did not become worthy of you.

For (γάρ) if he had been worthy (ἄξιος), [he would] not [have tasted]

34 death. (86) Jesus said: [The foxes]

96 [have] the[ir holes] and the birds have

2 [their] nest, but (δέ) the Son of Man

has no place to lay his head and

4 to rest. (87) Jesus said: Wretched (ταλαίπωρον)

is the body (σῶμα) which depends upon a body (σῶμα),

6 and wretched (ταλαίπωρος) is the soul (ψυχή) which depends

upon these two. (88) Jesus said: The angels (ἄγγελος)

8 and the prophets (προφήτης) will come to you and they

will give you what is yours. And

10 you, too, give to them what is in your hands,

and say to yourselves: "On which

12 day will they come and receive what is theirs?"

(89) Jesus said: Why do you wash the outside

14 of the cup (ποτήριον)? Do you not understand (νοεῖν) that

he who made the inside is also he

16 who made the outside? (90) Jesus said:

Come to Me, for easy (χρηστός)

18 is My yoke and My lordship is gentle,

and you shall find repose (ἀνάπαυσις) for yourselves.

20 (91) They said to Him: Tell us

who Thou art so that (ἵνα) we may believe (πιστεύειν) in Thee.

7 "The angels", or "The messengers".

47

ⲉⲣⲓⲥⲉ ⲛⲧⲁⲣⲉⲥⲡⲱϧ ⲉⲣⲟⲧⲛ ⲉⲡⲉⲥⲛⲉⲓ

14 ⲁⲥⲕⲁ ⲡϭⲗⲙⲉⲉⲓ ⲁⲡⲉⲥⲏⲧ ⲁⲥϧⲉ ⲉⲣⲟϥ ⲉϥ'

ϣⲟⲩⲉⲓⲧ' (98) ⲡⲉϫⲉ ⲓ̅ⲥ̅ ⲧⲙⲛⲧⲉⲣⲟ ⲙⲡⲉⲓⲱⲧ'

16 ⲉⲥⲧⲛⲧⲱⲛ ⲉⲩⲣⲱⲙⲉ ⲉϥⲟⲩⲱϣ ⲉⲙⲟⲩⲧ

ⲟⲩⲣⲱⲙⲉ ⲙⲙⲉⲅⲓⲥⲧⲁⲛⲟⲥ ⲁϥϣⲱⲗⲙ' ⲛ̅

18 ⲧⲥⲏϥⲉ ϧ̅ⲙ ⲡⲉϥⲛⲉⲓ ⲁϥϫⲟⲧⲥ̅ ⲛ̅ⲧϫⲟ ϫⲉ

ⲕⲁⲁⲥ ⲉϥⲛⲁⲉⲓⲙⲉ ϫⲉ ⲧⲉϥϭⲓϫ' ⲛⲁⲧⲱⲕ'

20 ⲉⲣⲟⲧⲛ ⲧⲟⲧⲉ ⲁϥϧⲱⲧⲃ̅ ⲙⲡⲙⲉⲅⲓⲥⲧⲁⲛⲟⲥ

(99) ⲡⲉϫⲉ ⲙ̅ⲙⲁⲑⲏⲧⲏⲥ ⲛⲁϥ ϫⲉ ⲛⲉⲕⲥⲛⲏⲧ

22 ⲙⲛ̅ ⲧⲉⲕⲙⲁⲁⲩ ⲥⲉⲁϧⲉⲣⲁⲧⲟⲩ ϧⲓ ⲡⲥⲁ ⲛ̅

ⲃⲟⲗ ⲡⲉϫⲁϥ ⲛⲁⲩ ϫⲉ ⲛⲉⲧⲛⲛⲉⲉⲓⲙⲁ

24 ⲉⲧⲣⲉ ⲙ̅ⲡⲟⲩⲱϣ ⲙ̅ⲡⲁⲉⲓⲱⲧ' ⲛⲁⲉⲓ ⲛⲉ

ⲛⲁⲥⲛⲏⲧ ⲙⲛ̅ ⲧⲁⲙⲁⲁⲩ ⲛⲧⲟⲟⲩ ⲡⲉ ⲉⲧⲛⲁ

26 ⲃⲱⲕ' ⲉϧⲟⲩⲛ ⲉⲧⲙⲛⲧⲉⲣⲟ ⲙ̅ⲡⲁⲉⲓⲱⲧ'

(100) ⲁⲩⲧⲥⲉⲃⲉ ⲓ̅ⲥ̅ ⲁⲩⲛⲟⲩⲃ ⲁⲩⲱ ⲡⲉϫⲁⲩ ⲛⲁϥ'

28 ϫⲉ ⲛⲉⲧⲏⲡ' ⲁⲕⲁⲓⲥⲁⲣ' ⲥⲉϣⲓⲧⲉ ⲙ̅ⲙⲟⲛ ⲛ̅

ⲛ̅ϣⲱⲙ' ⲡⲉϫⲁϥ ⲛⲁⲩ ϫⲉ ϯ ⲛⲁ ⲕⲁⲓⲥⲁⲣ'

30 ⲛ̅ⲕⲁⲓⲥⲁⲣ ϯ ⲛⲁ ⲡⲛⲟⲩⲧⲉ ⲙ̅ⲡⲛⲟⲩⲧⲉ

ⲁⲩⲱ ⲡⲉⲧⲉ ⲡⲱⲉⲓ ⲡⲉ ⲙⲁⲧⲛ̅ ⲛⲁⲉⲓϥ

32 (101) ⲡⲉⲧⲁⲙⲉⲥⲧⲉ ⲡⲉϥⲉⲓ[ⲱⲧ ⲁ]ⲛ ⲙⲛ̅ ⲧⲉϥ'

ⲙⲁⲁⲩ ⲛ̅ⲧⲁϧⲉ ϥⲛⲁϣ ⲣ̅ ⲙ̅[ⲁⲑⲏⲧⲏ]ⲥ ⲛⲁⲉⲓ ⲁ̅

34 ⲁⲩⲱ ⲡⲉⲧⲁⲙⲣ̅ⲣⲉ ⲡⲉ[ϥⲉⲓⲱⲧ ⲁⲛ ⲙ]ⲛ̅ ⲧⲉϥ

ⲙⲁⲁⲩ ⲛ̅ⲧⲁϧⲉ ϥⲛⲁϣ ⲣ̅ ⲙ̅[ⲁⲑⲏⲧⲏⲥ ⲛⲁ]

36 ⲉⲓ ⲁⲛ ⲧⲁⲙⲁⲁⲩ ⲅⲁⲣ ⲛⲧⲁ[

98 ⲉⲃ]ⲟⲗ [ⲧⲁⲙⲁⲁⲩ] ϫⲉ ⲙ̅ⲙⲉ ⲁⲥϯ ⲛⲁⲉⲓ ⲙ̅ⲡⲱⲛϧ

2 (102) ⲡⲉϫⲉ ⲓ̅ⲥ̅ [ϫⲉ ⲟ]ⲩⲟⲉⲓ ⲛⲁⲩ ⲙ̅ⲫⲁⲣⲓⲥⲁⲓⲟⲥ ϫⲉ

33 ⲛⲧⲁϧⲉ: ⲉ added above the line

50

accident. After she came into her house,

14 she put the jar down, she found it empty.

(98) Jesus said: The Kingdom of the Father

16 is like a man who wishes to kill

a powerful (μεγιστᾶνος) man. He drew

18 the sword in his house, he stuck it into the wall,

in order to know whether his hand would carry through;

20 then (τότε) he slew the powerful (μεγιστᾶνος) (man).

(99) The disciples (μαθητής) said to Him: Thy brethren

22 and Thy mother are standing outside.

He said to them: Those here

24 who do the will of My Father, they are

My brethren and My mother; these are they who shall

26 enter the Kingdom of My Father.

(100) They showed Jesus a gold (coin) and said to Him:

28 Caesar's men ask taxes from us.

He said to them: Give the things of Caesar

30 to Caesar, give the things of God to God

and give Me what is Mine.

32 (101) ‹ Jesus said:› Whoever does not hate his father and his

mother in My way will not be able to be a [disciple (μαθητής)] to me.

34 And whoever does [not] love [his father] and his

mother in My way will not be able to be a [disciple (μαθητής)]

36 to me, for (γάρ) My mother [   ]

98   but (δέ) [My] true [Mother] gave me the Life.

2 (102) Jesus said: Woe to them, the Pharisees (Φαρισαῖος), for

98 ⲉⲧⲉⲓⲛⲉ [ⲛ]ⲟⲩⲟⲩϩⲟⲣ· ⲉϥⲛ̅ⲕⲟⲧⲕ̅' ϩⲓϫⲛ̅ ⲛⲟⲩ

4 ⲟⲛⲉϥ· ⲛ̅[ϩⲉⲛ]ⲉϩⲟⲟⲩ ϫⲉ ⲟⲩⲧⲉ ϥⲟⲩⲱⲙ ⲁⲛ

ⲟⲩⲧⲉ ϥⲕ[ⲱ ⲁ]ⲛ ⲛ̅ⲛⲉϩⲟⲟⲩ ⲉⲟⲩⲱⲙ (103) ⲡⲉϫⲉ ⲓ̅ⲥ̅

6 ϫⲉ ⲟⲩⲙ̅[ⲁⲕⲁ]ⲣⲓⲟⲥ ⲡⲉ ⲡⲣⲱⲙⲉ ⲡⲁⲉⲓ ⲉⲧⲥⲟⲟⲩ̅

ϫⲉ ϩ[ⲛ̅ ⲁϣ] ⲙ̅ⲙⲉⲣⲟⲥ ⲉⲛⲗ̅ⲏⲥⲧⲏⲥ ⲛⲏⲩ ⲉϩⲟⲩ̅

8 ϣⲓⲛ[ⲁ ⲉϥⲛ̅]ⲁⲧⲱⲟⲩⲛ̅' ⲛ̅ϥⲥⲱⲟⲩϩ ⲛ̅ⲧⲉϥ'

ⲙ̅ⲛ̅ⲧ⁎[.] ⲁⲩⲱ ⲛ̅ϥⲙⲟⲩⲣ ⲙ̅ⲙⲟϥ ⲉϫⲛ̅ ⲧⲉϥ'

10 ϯⲡⲉ [ϩⲁ] ⲧⲉϥ̅ϩ ⲉⲙⲡⲁⲧⲟⲩⲉⲓ ⲉϩⲟⲩⲛ (104) ⲡⲉ

ϫⲁⲩ [ⲛⲁϥ] ϫⲉ ⲁⲙⲟⲩ ⲛ̅ⲧⲛ̅ϣⲗ̅ⲏⲗ' ⲙ̅ⲡⲟⲟⲩ

12 ⲁⲩⲱ ⲛ̅ⲧⲛ̅ⲣⲛⲏⲥⲧⲉⲩⲉ ⲡⲉϫⲉ ⲓ̅ⲥ̅ ϫⲉ ⲟⲩ ⲅⲁⲣ'

ⲡⲉ ⲡⲛⲟⲃⲉ ⲛ̅ⲧⲁⲉⲓⲁⲁϥ' ⲏ ⲛ̅ⲧⲁⲩϫⲣⲟ ⲉⲣⲟⲉⲓ

14 ϩⲛ̅ ⲟⲩ ⲁⲗⲗⲁ ϩⲟⲧⲁⲛ ⲉⲣϣⲁⲛⲡⲛⲩⲙⲫⲓⲟⲥ ⲉⲓ

ⲉⲃⲟⲗ ϩⲙ̅ ⲡⲛⲩⲙⲫⲱⲛ ⲧⲟⲧⲉ ⲙⲁⲣⲟⲩⲛ̅ⲏ'

16 ⲥⲧⲉⲩⲉ ⲁⲩⲱ ⲙⲁⲣⲟⲩϣⲗ̅ⲏⲗ' (105) ⲡⲉϫⲉ ⲓ̅ⲥ̅ ϫⲉ ⲡⲉ

ⲧⲛⲁⲥⲟⲩⲱⲛ ⲡⲉⲓⲱⲧ ⲙⲛ̅ ⲧⲙⲁⲁⲩ ⲥⲉⲛⲁⲙⲟⲩ

18 ⲧⲉ ⲉⲣⲟϥ' ϫⲉ ⲡϣⲏⲣⲉ ⲙ̅ⲡⲟⲣⲛⲏ (106) ⲡⲉϫⲉ ⲓ̅ⲥ̅ ϫⲉ

ϩⲟⲧⲁⲛ ⲉⲧⲉⲧⲛ̅ϣⲁⲣ ⲡⲥⲛⲁⲩ ⲟⲩⲁ ⲧⲉⲧⲛⲁϣ

20 ⲡⲉ ⲛ̅ϣⲏⲣⲉ ⲙ̅ⲡⲣⲱⲙⲉ ⲁⲩⲱ ⲉⲧⲉⲧⲛ̅ϣⲁⲛ

ϫⲟⲟⲥ ϫⲉ ⲡⲧⲟⲟⲩ ⲡⲱⲱⲛⲉ ⲉⲃⲟⲗ· ϥⲛⲁ

22 ⲡⲱⲱⲛⲉ (107) ⲡⲉϫⲉ ⲓ̅ⲥ̅ ϫⲉ ⲧⲙ̅ⲛ̅ⲧⲉⲣⲟ ⲉⲥⲛ̅ⲧⲱ

ⲉⲩⲣⲱⲙⲉ ⲛ̅ϣⲱⲥ ⲉⲩⲛ̅ⲧⲁϥ' ⲙ̅ⲙⲁⲩ ⲛ̅ϣⲉ ⲛ̅

24 ⲉⲥⲟⲟⲩ ⲁⲟⲩⲁ ⲛ̅ϩⲏⲧⲟⲩ ⲥⲱⲣⲙ̅' ⲉⲡⲛⲟϭ ⲡⲉ

ⲁϥⲕⲱ ⲙ̅ⲡⲥⲧⲉⲯⲓⲧ ⲁϥϣⲓⲛⲉ ⲛ̅ⲥⲁ ⲡⲓⲟⲩⲁ'

26 ϣⲁⲛⲧⲉϥϩⲉ ⲉⲣⲟϥ· ⲛ̅ⲧⲁⲣⲉϥϩⲓⲥⲉ ⲡⲉϫⲁϥ'

8 ⲥⲱⲟⲩϩ: after ⲱ there is ϩ cancelled by a horizontal stroke

they are like a dog sleeping in the

4 manger of oxen, for neither (οὔτε) does he eat

nor (οὔτε) does he allow the oxen to eat. (103) Jesus said:

6 Blessed (μακάριος) is the man who knows

i[n which] part (μέρος) (of the night) the robbers (λῃστής) will come in,

8 so that (ἵνα) he will rise and collect his

[   ] and gird up his loins

10 before they come in.

(104) They said [to Him]: Come and let us pray today

12 and let us fast (νηστεύειν). Jesus said: Which then (γάρ)

is the sin that I have committed, or (ἤ) in what have I been vanquished?

14 But (ἀλλά) when (ὅταν) the bridegroom (νύμφιος) comes

out of the bridal chamber (νυμφών), then (τότε) let them

16 fast (νηστεύειν) and let them pray. (105) Jesus said:

Whoever knows father and mother shall be called

18 the son of a harlot (πόρνη). (106) Jesus said:

When (ὅταν) you make the two one, you shall become

20 sons of Man, and when you

say: "Mountain, be moved", it will

22 be moved. (107) Jesus said: The Kingdom is like

a shepherd who had a hundred

24 sheep. One of them went astray, which was the largest.

He left behind ninety-nine, he sought for the one

26 until he found it. Having tired himself out, he said

ⲙ̄ⲡⲉⲥⲟⲟⲩ ⲍⲉ ϯⲟⲩⲟϣⲕ· ⲡⲁⲣⲁ ⲡⲥⲧⲉⲯⲓⲧ'

28 (108) ⲡⲉⲍⲉ ⲓ̄ⲥ̄ ⲍⲉ ⲡⲉⲧⲁⲥⲱ ⲉⲃⲟⲗ ϩⲛ̄ ⲧⲁⲧⲁⲡⲣⲟ

ϥⲛⲁϣⲱⲡⲉ ⲛ̄ⲧⲁϩⲉ ⲁⲛⲟⲕ ϩⲱ ϯⲛⲁϣⲱⲡⲉ

30 ⲉⲛⲧⲟϥ ⲡⲉ ⲁⲩⲱ ⲛⲉⲑⲏⲡ· ⲛⲁⲟⲩⲱⲛϩ ⲉⲣⲟϥ'

(109) ⲡⲉⲍⲉ ⲓ̄ⲥ̄ ⲍⲉ ⲧⲙ̄ⲛⲧⲉⲣⲟ ⲉⲥⲧⲛ̄ⲧⲱⲛ ⲉⲩⲣⲱ

32 ⲙⲉ ⲉⲩⲛⲧⲁϥ [ⲙ̄ⲙ]ⲁⲩ ϩⲛ̄ ⲧⲉϥⲥⲱϣⲉ ⲛ̄ⲛⲟⲩ

ⲉϩⲟ ⲉϥϩⲟ[ⲏⲡ ⲉϥ]ⲟ ⲛ̄ⲁⲧⲥⲟⲟⲩⲛ' ⲉⲣⲟϥ ⲁⲩ

34 ⲱ ⲙ̄[ⲛ̄ⲛⲥⲁ ⲧ]ⲣⲉϥⲙⲟⲩ ⲁϥⲕⲁⲁϥ ⲙ̄ⲡⲉϥ'

[ϣⲏⲣⲉ ⲛⲉⲡ]ϣⲏⲣⲉ ⲥⲟⲟⲩⲛ ⲁⲛ ⲁϥϥⲓ'

99 ⲧⲥⲱϣⲉ ⲉⲧⲙ̄ⲙⲁⲩ ⲁϥⲧⲁⲁ[ϥ ⲉⲃⲟⲗ] ⲁⲩⲱ ⲡⲉⲛ

2 ⲧⲁϩⲧⲟⲟⲩⲥ ⲁϥⲉⲓ ⲉϥⲥⲕⲁⲓ [ⲁϥϩⲉ] ⲁⲡⲉϩⲟ ⲁϥ

ⲁⲣⲭⲉⲓ ⲛ̄ϯ ϩⲟⲙⲧ' ⲉⲧⲙ̄ⲛⲥⲉ ⲛ̄[ⲛⲉⲧ]ϥⲟⲩⲁϣⲟⲩ

4 (110) ⲡⲉⲍⲉ ⲓ̄ⲥ̄ ⲍⲉ ⲡⲉⲛⲧⲁϩϭⲓⲛⲉ [ⲙ̄ⲡ]ⲕⲟⲥⲙⲟⲥ

ⲛϥ̄ⲣ ⲣⲙⲙⲁⲟ ⲙⲁⲣⲉϥⲁⲣⲛⲁ ⲙ̄ⲡⲕⲟⲥⲙⲟⲥ

6 (111) ⲡⲉⲍⲉ ⲓ̄ⲥ̄ ⲍⲉ ⲙ̄ⲡⲏⲩⲉ ⲛⲁϭⲱⲗ ⲁⲩⲱ ⲡⲕⲁϩ

ⲙ̄ⲡⲉⲧⲛ̄ⲙⲧⲟ ⲉⲃⲟⲗ' ⲁⲩⲱ ⲡⲉⲧⲟⲛϩ ⲉⲃⲟⲗ ϩⲛ̄

8 ⲡⲉⲧⲟⲛϩ ϥⲛⲁⲛⲁⲩ ⲁⲛ ⲉⲙⲟⲩ ⲟⲩⲁ ϩⲟⲧⲓ ⲉⲓⲥ

ⲍⲱ ⲙ̄ⲙⲟⲥ ⲍⲉ ⲡⲉⲧⲁϩⲉ ⲉⲣⲟϥ' ⲟⲩⲁⲁϥ ⲡⲕⲟⲥ

10 ⲙⲟⲥ ⲙ̄ⲡϣⲁ ⲙ̄ⲙⲟϥ' ⲁⲛ (112) ⲡⲉⲍⲉ ⲓ̄ⲥ̄ ⲍⲉ ⲟⲩⲟⲉⲓ

ⲛ̄ⲧⲥⲁⲣⲝ' ⲧⲁⲉⲓ ⲉⲧⲟϣⲉ ⲛ̄ⲧⲯⲩⲭⲏ ⲟⲩⲟⲉⲓ

12 ⲛ̄ⲧⲯⲩⲭⲏ ⲧⲁⲉⲓ ⲉⲧⲟϣⲉ ⲛ̄ⲧⲥⲁⲣⲝ (113) ⲡⲉⲍⲁⲩ

ⲛⲁϥ ⲛ̄ϭⲓ ⲛⲉϥⲙⲁⲑⲏⲧⲏⲥ ⲍⲉ ⲧⲙ̄ⲛⲧⲉⲣⲟ

14 ⲉⲥⲛ̄ⲛⲏⲩ ⲛⲁϣ ⲛ̄ϩⲟⲟⲩ ⲉⲥⲛ̄ⲛⲏⲩ ⲁⲛ ϩⲛ̄ ⲟⲩ

27 ⲉⲥⲟⲟⲩ: ⲉⲥⲟⲩⲟ has been corrected by cancelling ⲩ and adding ⲩ after
the second ⲟ above the line

32 ϩⲛ̄: ϩ added above the line

6 ⲁⲩⲱ *sic*; *l.* ⲙⲛ

8 ⲟⲩⲁ ϩⲟⲧⲓ *sic*; *l.* ⲟⲩⲇⲉ ⲉϩⲟⲧⲉ ϩⲟⲧⲓ (haplography)

to the sheep: I love thee more than (παρά) ninety-nine.

28 (108) Jesus said: Whoever drinks from My mouth

shall become as I am and I myself will become

30 he, and the hidden things shall be revealed to him.

(109) Jesus said: The Kingdom is like a man

32 who had a

treasure [hidden] in his field, without knowing it.

34 And [after] he died, he left it to his

[son. The] son did not know (about it), he accepted

99 that field, he sold [it]. And he who bought it,

2 he went, while he was plowing [he found] the treasure.

He began (ἄρχεσθαι) to lend money to whomever he wished.

4 (110) Jesus said: Whoever has found the world (κόσμος)

and become rich, let him deny (ἀρνεῖσθαι) the world (κόσμος).

6 (111) Jesus said: The heavens will be rolled up and the earth

in your presence, and he who lives on

8 the Living (One) shall see neither death nor (οὐδέ) <fear>, because (ὅτι)

Jesus says: Whoever finds himself,

10 of him the world (κόσμος) is not worthy. (112) Jesus said: Woe

to the flesh (σάρξ) which depends upon the soul (ψυχή); woe

12 to the soul (ψυχή) which depends upon the flesh (σάρξ).

(113) His disciples (μαθητής) said to Him:

14 When will the Kingdom come? < Jesus said:> It will not come by

6 Ms. literally: "and the earth is in your presence".

99 ϭⲱϣⲧ' ⲉⲃⲟⲗ' ⲉⲧⲛⲁϫⲟⲟⲥ ⲁⲛ ϫⲉ ⲉⲓⲥ ϩⲏⲏ

16 ⲧⲉ ⲙ̄ⲡⲓⲥⲁ ⲏ ⲉⲓⲥ ϩⲏⲏⲧⲉ ⲧⲏ ⲁⲗⲗⲁ ⲧⲙ̄ⲛⲧⲉⲣⲟ

ⲙ̄ⲡⲉⲓⲱⲧ' ⲉⲥⲡⲟⲣϣ' ⲉⲃⲟⲗ ϩⲓϫⲙ̄ ⲡⲕⲁϩ ⲁⲩⲱ

18 ⲣ̄ⲣⲱⲙⲉ ⲛⲁⲩ ⲁⲛ ⲉⲣⲟⲥ (114) ⲡⲉϫⲉ ⲥⲓⲙⲱⲛ ⲡⲉⲧⲣⲟⲥ

ⲛⲁⲩ ϫⲉ ⲙⲁⲣⲉⲙⲁⲣⲓϩⲁⲙ ⲉⲓ ⲉⲃⲟⲗ ⲛ̄ϩⲏⲧⲛ̄

20 ϫⲉ ⲛ̄ⲥϩⲓⲟⲙⲉ ⲙ̄ⲡϣⲁ ⲁⲛ' ⲙ̄ⲡⲱⲛϩ ⲡⲉϫⲉ ⲓ̄ⲥ

ϫⲉ ⲉⲓⲥ ϩⲏⲏⲧⲉ ⲁⲛⲟⲕ' ϯⲛⲁⲥⲱⲕ' ⲙ̄ⲙⲟⲥ ϫⲉ

22 ⲕⲁⲁⲥ ⲉⲉⲓⲛⲁⲁⲥ ⲛ̄ϩⲟⲟⲩⲧ' ϣⲓⲛⲁ ⲉⲥⲛⲁϣⲱ

ⲡⲉ ϩⲱⲱⲥ ⲛⲟⲩⲡⲛ̄ⲁ ⲉϥⲟⲛϩ ⲉϥⲉⲓⲛⲉ ⲙ̄

24 ⲙⲱⲧⲛ̄ ⲛ̄ϩⲟⲟⲩⲧ ϫⲉ ⲥϩⲓⲙⲉ ⲛⲓⲙ' ⲉⲥⲛⲁⲁⲥ'

ⲛ̄ϩⲟⲟⲩⲧ' ⲥⲛⲁⲃⲱⲕ' ⲉϩⲟⲩⲛ ⲉⲧⲙⲛ̄ⲧⲉⲣⲟ

26 ⲛ̄ⲙⲡⲏⲩⲉ ⟨ ⟨ ⟨ ⟨ ⟨ ⟨ ⟨ ⟨ ⟨ ⟨ ⟨ ⟨ ⟨

ⲡⲉⲩⲁⲅⲅⲉⲗⲓⲟⲛ

28 ⲡⲕⲁⲧⲁ ⲑⲱⲙⲁⲥ

expectation; they will not say: "See,

16 here", or (ἤ): "See, there". But (ἀλλά) the Kingdom
of the Father is spread upon the earth and

18 men do not see it. (114) Simon Peter said
to them: Let Mary go out from among us,

20 because women are not worthy of the Life. Jesus said:
See, I shall lead her,

22 so that I will make her male, that (ἵνα)
she too may become a living spirit (πνεῦμα), resembling

24 you males. For every woman who makes herself
male will enter the Kingdom

26 of Heaven.

The Gospel (εὐαγγέλιον)

28 according to (κατά) Thomas

SCRIPTURAL PARALLELS AND ECHOES

Log. 1, pl. 80, 12-14: cf. *Jn.* VIII, 51 and 52.

Log. 2, pl. 80, 14-16: cf., in one sense, *Mt.* VII, 7-8 = *Lk.* XI, 9-10.

Log. 3, pl. 80, 19-24: cf., in one sense, *Deut.* XXX, 11-14 and *Rom.* X, 6-8; pl. 80, 25: *Lk.* XVII, 21*b*.

Log. 4, pl. 81, 6-8: cf., in one sense, *Mt.* XI, 25 = *Lk.* X, 21; pl. 81, 9-10: *Mt.* XIX, 30 et XX, 16 = *Mk.* X, 31 = *Lk.* XIII, 30.

Log. 5, pl. 81, 13: *Lk.* VIII, 17 (= *Mk.* IV, 22); cf. *Mt.* X, 26 = *Lk.* XII, 2.

Log. 6, pl. 81, 15-18: cf. *Mt.* VI, 1-18; pl. 81, 18: cf. *Eph.* IV, 25 and *Col.* III, 9; pl. 81, 19: cf., in one sense, *Mt.* VII, 12 = *Lk.* VI, 31; pl. 81, 21-23: *Mt.* X, 26 = *Lk.* XII, 2 (cf. *Mk.* IV, 22 = *Lk.* VIII, 17).

Log. 8, pl. 81, 29-pl. 82, 2: cf. *Mt.* XIII, 47-50; pl. 82, 2-3: *Mt.* XI, 15, XIII, 9 and 43; *Mk.* IV, 9 and 23, VII, 16; *Lk.* VIII, 8, XIV, 35; *Rev.* II, 7, XIII, 9.

Log. 9, pl. 82, 3-13: *Mt.* XIII, 3-9 = *Mk.* IV, 3-9 = *Lk.* VIII, 5-8.

Log. 10, pl. 82, 14-16: cf. *Lk.* XII, 49.

Log. 11, pl. .82, 16-17: cf. *Mt.* XXIV, 35 = *Mk.* XIII, 31 = *Lk.* XXI, 33; *Mt.* V, 18 = *Lk.* XVI, 17; *I Cor.* VII, 31; *I Jn.* II, 17.

Log. 12, pl. 82, 26-27: cf., perhaps, *Mt.* XVIII, 1 = *Mk.* IX, 34 = *Lk.* IX, 46.

Log. 13, pl. 82, 30-pl. 83, 4: cf., in one sense, *Mt.* XVI, 13-16 = *Mk.* VIII, 27-30 = *Lk.* IX, 18-21; pl. 83, 5: cf. *Mt.* XXIII, 8 and, perhaps, *Jn.* XV, 15; pl. 83, 6: cf. *Jn.* IV, 10-14; pl. 83, 7: cf. *Lk.* IX, 10; pl. 83, 12-13: cf. *Jn.* VIII, 59 and X, 31.

Log. 14, pl. 83, 19-23: *Lk.* X, 8-9 (cf. *Mt.* X, 8; *I Cor.* X, 27); pl. 83, 24-27: *Mt.* XV, 11 = *Mk.* VII, 15.

Log. 16, pl. 83, 31- pl. 84, 3: *Lk.* XII, 49 and 51-53; cf. *Mt.* X, 34-36.

Log. 17, pl. 84, 5-9: cf. *I Cor.* II, 9 (quoting *Is.* LXIV, 3).

Log. 19, pl. 84, 19: cf., perhaps, *Jn.* XIII, 35 and XV, 8; pl. 84, 20-21: cf., perhaps, *Mt.* III, 9 = *Lk.* III, 8 or *Mt.* IV, 3 = *Lk.* IV, 3; pl. 84, 21-25: cf., in one sense, *Rev.* II, 7.

Log. 20, pl. 84, 26-33: *Mk.* IV, 30-32; cf. *Mt.* XIII, 31-32 and *Lk.* XIII, 18-19.

Log. 21, pl. 85, 4-5: cf., perhaps, *II Cor.* V, 3; pl. 85, 7-14: *Mt.* XXIV, 43-44 = *Lk.* XII, 39-40 (cf. *Mt.* VI, 19-20); pl. 85, 10: cf. *Mt.* XII, 29 = *Mk.* III, 27 = *Lk.* XI, 21-22; pl. 85, 11-12: *Lk.* XII, 35 and 37 (cf. *Mt.* XXV, 13); pl. 85, 17-18: cf. *Mk.* IV, 29 (*Joel* III, 13); pl. 85, 19: *Mt.* XI, 15, XIII, 9 and 43; *Mk.* IV, 9 and 23, VII, 16; *Lk.* VIII, 8, XIV, 35; *Rev.* II, 7, XIII, 9.

59

Log. 22, pl. 85, 20-22: *Mt.* xviii, 1-3 (cf. *Mk.* ix, 36 and *Lk.* ix, 47-48); compare also *Mt.* xix, 13-15 = *Mk.* x, 13-15 = *Lk.* xviii, 15-17; pl. 85, 28-31: cf. *Gal.* iii, 28, *Eph.* ii, 14-16.

Log. 23, pl. 86, 1-2: cf. *Mt.* xxii, 14; *Jn.* vi, 70, xiii, 18, xv, 16 and 19.

Log. 24, pl. 86, 4-6: cf., perhaps, *Jn.* xiv, 4-5; pl. 86, 6-7: *Mt.* xi, 15, xiii, 9 and 43; *Mk.* iv, 9 and 23, vii, 16; *Lk.* viii, 8, xiv, 35; *Rev.* ii, 7, xiii, 9; pl. 86, 7-10: compare, perhaps, *Mt.* vi, 22-23 = *Lk.* xi, 34-35.

Log. 25, pl. 86, 10-11: *Mt.* xix, 19*b* and xxii, 39 = *Mk.* xii, 31 = *Lk.* x, 27 (= *Lev.* xix, 18, quoted also by *Jam.* ii, 8); pl. 86, 12: cf. *Deut.* xxxii, 10, *Ps.* xvii, 8, *Prov.* vii, 2, *Eccles.* xvii, 22.

Log. 26, pl. 86, 12-17: *Mt.* vii, 3-5 = *Lk.* vi, 41-42.

Log. 27, pl. 86, 18-19: cf., perhaps, *Mt.* vi, 33 = *Lk.* xii, 31; pl. 86, 20: cf. *Jn.* xiv, 9 and *Mt.* v, 8.

Log. 28, pl. 86, 22: cf. *I Tim.* iii, 16.

Log. 30, pl. 87, 3-5: cf. *Mt.* xviii, 20.

Log. 31, pl. 87, 5-7: *Mt.* xiii, 57 = *Mk.* vi, 4; *Lk.* iv, 23-24; *Jn.* iv, 44.

Log. 32, pl. 87, 8-10: *Mt.* v, 14*b*; cf. *Mt.* vii, 24-25 and *Is.* ii, 2.

Log. 33, pl. 87, 10-13: *Mt.* x, 27 = *Lk.* xii, 3; pl. 87, 13-17: *Mk.* iv, 21 = *Lk.* viii, 16; *Mt.* v, 15 = *Lk.* xi, 33.

Log. 34, pl. 87, 18-20: *Mt.* xv, 14, *Lk.* vi, 39.

Log. 35, pl. 87, 20-24: *Mt.* xii, 29 = *Mk.* iii, 27; cf. *Lk.* xi, 21-22.

Log. 36, pl. 87, 24-27: *Mt.* vi, 25 = *Lk.* xii, 22; cf. *Mt.* vi, 31 = *Lk.* xii, 29.

Log. 37, pl. 87, 27-29: cf. *Jn.* xiv, 22 and *I Jn.* iii, 2; pl. 87, 30-31: cf., in one sense, *Gen.* ii, 25 and iii, 7; pl. 88, 1: cf. *Mt.* xvi, 16.

Log. 38, pl. 88, 2-5: cf., perhaps, *Mt.* xiii, 17 = *Lk.* x, 24; pl. 88, 5-6: cf. *Mt.* ix, 15, *Mk.* ii, 20, *Lk.* v, 35 and xxi, 6; pl. 88, 6-7: cf. *Jn.* vii, 33-34 and 36.

Log. 39, pl. 88, 7-11: *Mt.* xxiii, 13 = *Lk.* xi, 52; pl. 88, 11-13: *Mt.* x, 16.

Log. 40, pl. 88, 13-16: cf. *Mt.* xv, 13 and *Jn.* xv, 1-10.

Log. 41, pl. 88, 16-18: *Mt.* xiii, 12 = *Mk.* iv, 25 = *Lk.* viii, 18; cf. *Mt.* xxv, 29 = *Lk.* xix, 26.

Log. 43, pl. 88, 20-22: cf. *Jn.* xiv, 8-11; pl. 88, 24-26: cf. *Mt.* xii, 33 = *Lk.* vi, 43-44; *Mt.* vii, 17-20.

Log. 44, pl. 88, 26-32: *Mt.* xii, 31-32 = *Mk.* iii, 28-29 = *Lk.* xii, 10.

Log. 45, pl. 88, 31-pl. 89, 5: *Lk.* vi, 44-45 = *Mt.* vii, 16 + xii, 35 + xii, 34.

Log. 46, pl. 89, 6-12: *Mt.* xi, 11 = *Lk.* vii, 28.

Log. 47, pl. 89, 14-17: *Mt.* vi, 24 = *Lk.* xvi, 13; pl. 89, 17-19: *Lk.* v, 39; pl. 89, 19-23: *Mt.* ix, 16-17 = *Mk.* ii, 21-22 = *Lk.* v, 36-38.

Log. 48, pl. 89, 24-25: *Mt.* xviii, 19 (cf., perhaps, *Mt.* xii, 25 = *Mk.* iii, 25); pl. 89, 25-27: *Mt.* xvii, 20 (cf. *Mt.* xxi, 21 = *Mk.* xi, 22-23). Cf. *I Cor.* xiii, 2.

Log. 50, pl. 90, 3: cf. *Lk.* xvi, 8, *Jn.* xii, 36, *Eph.* v, 8, *I Thess.* v, 5; pl. 90, 4: cf. *Jn.* vi, 57, *Rom.* ix, 26.

Log. 51, pl. 90, 11: cf., in one sense, *Mt.* xvii, 11-12, or *Jn.* v, 25.

Log. 52, pl. 90, 12-18: cf., in one sense, *Jn.* v, 39-40 and viii, 53; moreover, *Lk.* xxiv, 5 and *Mt.* viii, 22 = *Lk.* ix, 60.

Log. 53, pl. 90, 19: cf. *Rom.* ii, 25 and iii, 1; pl. 90, 22: cf. *Rom.* ii, 29.

Log. 54, pl. 90, 23-24: *Mt.* v, 3 = *Lk.* vi, 20.

Log. 55, pl. 90, 25-29: *Mt.* x, 37-38 = *Lk.* xiv, 26-27; cf. *Mt.* xvi, 24 = *Mk.* viii, 34 = *Lk.* ix, 23.

Log. 56, pl. 90, 32: cf. *Heb.* xi, 38.

Log. 57, pl. 90, 33-pl. 91, 7: *Mt.* xiii, 24-30.

Log. 58, pl. 91, 8-9: cf., in one sense, *Jam.* i, 12 and *I Pet.* iii, 14.

Log. 61, pl. 91, 23-25: *Lk.* xvii, 34 (cf. *Mt.* xxiv, 40-41); pl. 91, 29-30: cf. *Mt.* xi, 27 = *Lk.* x, 22, *Jn.* vi, 37 and 39, xvii, 2, 6 and 9; *Lk.* ii, 49.

Log. 62, pl. 92, 1-2: *Mt.* vi, 3.

Log. 63, pl. 92, 3-9: *Lk.* xii, 16-21; pl. 92, 9-10: *Mt.* xi, 15, xiii, 9 and 43; *Mk.* iv, 9 and 23, vii, 16; *Lk.* viii, 8, xiv, 35; *Rev.* ii, 7, xiii, 9.

Log. 64, pl. 92, 10-35: *Lc.* xiv, 16-24 = *Mt.* xxii, 2-10.

Log. 65, pl. 93, 1-15: *Mt.* xxi, 33-41 = *Mk.* xii, 1-8 = *Lk.* xx, 9-16; pl. 93, 16: *Mt.* xi, 15, xiii, 9 and 43; *Mk.* iv, 9 and 23, vii, 16; *Lk.* viii, 8, xiv, 35; *Rev.* ii, 7, xiii, 9.

Log. 66, pl. 93, 16-19: *Mt.* xxi, 42 (= *Ps.* cxvii, 22) = *Mk.* xii, 10 = *Lk.* xx, 17; cf. also *I Pet.* ii, 4-6.

Log. 67, pl. 93, 19-20: cf. *Mt.* xvi, 26 = *Mk.* viii, 36 = *Lk.* ix, 25.

Log. 68, pl. 93, 21-22: cf. *Mt.* v, 11 = *Lk.* vi, 22.

Log. 69, pl. 93, 25: cf. *Mt.* v, 10; pl. 93, 27: cf. *Mt.* xxii, 16, *Jn.* iv, 23 and 24, xvii, 17 and 19, etc.; pl. 93, 28: cf. *Mt.* v, 6 = *Lk.* vi, 21.

Log. 71, pl. 93, 34-35: cf., in one sense, *Mt.* xxvi, 61 (and xxvii, 40) *Mk.* xiv, 58; *Jn.* ii, 19; *Acts* vi, 14.

Log. 72, pl. 94, 1-6: *Lk.* xii, 13-14.

Log. 73, pl. 94, 6-9: *Mt.* ix, 37-38 = *Lk.* x, 2.

Log. 75, pl. 94, 11-13: cf., perhaps, *Mt.* xxii, 10-14, ix, 15 (= *Mk.* ii, 19 = *Lk.* v, 34; cf. *Jn.* iii, 29) and xxv, 10.

Log. 76, pl. 94, 14-19: *Mt.* xiii, 45-46; pl. 94, 19-20: cf. *Mt.* xiii, 44; pl. 94, 19-22: *Mt.* vi, 19-20 = *Lk.* xii, 33.

Log. 77, pl. 94, 23: cf. *Jn.* viii, 12; pl. 94, 25-26: cf. *Rom.* xi, 36, and *I Cor.* viii, 6.

Log. 78, pl. 94, 28-pl. 95, 2: *Mt.* xi, 7-8 = *Lk.* vii, 24-25; pl. 94, 32: *Rev.* vi, 15 (cf. *Ps.* ii, 2, *Is.* xxiv, 21) and *Mt.* xx, 25.

Log. 79, pl. 95, 3-8: *Lk.* xi, 27-28; pl. 95, 9-12: *Lk.* xxiii, 29. Cf. also *Mt.* xxiv, 19 = *Mk.* xiii, 17 = *Lk.* xxi, 23.

Log. 81, pl. 95, 15-16: cf. *I Cor.* iv, 8.

Log. 82, pl. 95, 17-19: cf., in one sense, *Mk.* xii, 34.

Log. 86, pl. 95, 34-pl. 96, 4: *Mt.* viii, 20 = *Lk.* ix, 58.

Log. 88, pl. 96, 7-9: cf. *Mt.* xvi, 27 = *Mk.* viii, 38*b* = *Lk.* ix, 26*b*.

Log. 89, pl. 96, 13-16: *Mt.* xxiii, 26 = *Lk.* xi, 39-40.

Log. 90, pl. 96, 17-19: *Mt.* xi, 28-30.

Log. 91, pl. 96, 21: cf. *Jn.* vi, 30; pl. 96, 22-25: *Lk.* xii, 56 = *Mt.* xvi, 3.

Log. 92, pl. 96, 26: cf., in one sense, *Mt.* vii, 7-8 = *Lk.* xi, 9-10.

Log. 93, pl. 96, 30-33: *Mt.* vii, 6.

Log. 94, pl. 96, 33-34: *Mt.* vii, 8 = *Lk.* xi, 10.

Log. 95, pl. 96, 35-pl. 97, 2: *Lk.* vi, 34-35 (cf. vi, 30 and *Mt.* v, 42).

Log. 96, pl. 97, 2-5: *Mt.* xiii, 33 = *Lk.* xiii, 20-21; pl. 97, 6: *Mt.* xi, 15, xiii, 9 and 43; *Mk.* iv, 9 and 23, vii, 16; *Lk.* viii, 8, xiv, 35; *Rev.* ii, 7, xiii, 9.

Log. 99, pl. 97, 21-26: *Mt.* xii, 47-50 = *Mk.* iii, 32-35 = *Lk.* viii, 20-21.

Log. 100, pl. 97, 27-30: *Mt.* xxii, 16-21 = *Mk.* xii, 13-17 = *Lk.* xx, 21-25.

Log. 101, pl. 97, 32-33: *Mt.* x, 37 = *Lk.* xiv, 26; cf. *Mt.* xix, 29 = *Mk.* x, 29 = *Lk.* xviii, 29*b*.

Log. 102, pl. 98, 2: cf. *Lk.* xi, 42 and 43, *Mt.* xxiii, 13, 14, 15, 23, 25, 27 and 29.

Log. 103, pl. 98, 6-8: cf. *Mt.* xxiv, 43 = *Lk.* xii, 39; pl. 98, 9-10: cf. *Lk.* xii, 35.

Log. 104, pl. 98, 10-16: *Mt.* ix, 14-15 = *Mk.* ii, 18-20 = *Lk.* v, 33-35.

Log. 105, pl. 98, 17-18: cf., perhaps, *Jn.* viii, 41.

Log. 107, pl. 98, 22-27: *Mt.* xviii, 12-13 = *Lk.* xv, 3-6.

Log. 108, pl. 98, 28-29: cf., in one sense, *Jn.* vii, 37.

Log. 109, pl. 98, 31-pl. 99, 3: cf. *Mt.* xiii, 44.

Log. 111, pl. 99, 6: cf. *Is.* xxxiv, 4, *Heb.* i, 12, *Rev.* vi, 14.

Log. 113, pl. 99, 12-18: *Lk.* xvii, 20-21; cf., perhaps, *Mt.* xxiv, 23 and *Jn.* i, 26.